He Is Jehovah

How Knowing the Names of God Encourages Women to Share His Faithfulness

By Jennifer Wake

Acknowledgments

Thank you to my wonderful husband, who encouraged me to follow my dream of writing and speaking about God. Thank you for working on all the formatting and never letting me give up. I love you more.

Thank you to my wonderful children, who taught me to be a better mom and Christian. I love you very much and am proud of all of you.

Thank you to my sisters, who have challenged me never to give up and to learn continuously. Thank you both for being such strong, independent women. I am blessed to be one of the "Miller Girls." I love you both so much.

To my editor, Liz Giertz, thank you for putting up with this new writer. Your tireless efforts moved me from thinking about publishing to doing it. Thank you for encouraging me and never giving up!

To Mary Frances Booth, thank you for believing in me, keeping me grounded, and speaking life into me for years.

To Beth Walter, thank you for making me laugh and speaking the Truth. I love you, friend!

To all my PWOC friends near and far, I pray for you to grow closer to God. Pursue Him with all your heart! Thank you to the PWOC Bible study groups that helped me grow as a writer.

Thank you to the IGNITE PWOC training team for helping me grow and develop as a trainer and a speaker.

To Andrea Plotner, who told me I was a writer so many years ago before I saw it in myself.

Copyright © 2024 by Jennifer Wake
All rights reserved.

No portion of this book may be reproduced in any form without written permission from the publisher or author except as permitted by U.S. copyright law. This publication is designed to provide accurate and authoritative information in regard to the subject matter covered. It is sold with the understanding that neither the author nor the publisher is engaged in rendering legal, investment, accounting, or other professional services. While the publisher and author have used their best efforts in preparing this book, they make no representations or warranties with respect to the accuracy or completeness of the contents of this book and expressly disclaim any implied warranties of merchantability or fitness for a particular purpose. No warranty may be created or extended by sales representatives or written sales materials. The advice and strategies contained herein may not be suitable for your situation. You should consult with a professional when appropriate. Neither the publisher nor the author shall be liable for any loss of profit or any other commercial damages, including but not limited to special, incidental, consequential, personal, or other damages.

Book cover by Abigail Harvey,
Illustrations by Unsplash
1st edition 2024

Table of Contents

Introduction	1
1. JEHOVAH: SELF-SUFFICIENT ONE	5
Prayers to Jehovah	19
Questions for Discussion	21
2. JEHOVAH-JIREH: THE LORD OUR PROVIDER	25
Prayers to Jehovah-Jireh	35
Questions for Discussion	37
3. JEHOVAH-RAPHA: THE LORD OUR HEALER	41
Prayers to Jehovah-Rapha	53
Questions for Discussion	55
4. JEHOVAH-RAAH: THE LORD OUR SHEPHERD	59
Prayers to Jehovah-Raah	69
Questions for Discussion	71
5. JEHOVAH SHALOM: THE LORD OUR PEACE	75
Prayers to Jehovah-Shalom	89
Questions for Discussion	91
6. JEHOVAH-MAGINNENU: THE LORD OUR SHEILD	95
Prayers to Jehovah-Maginnenu	109
Questions for Discussion	111
CHARLIE MIKE: CONTINUING THE MISSION	115
SAMPLE NAME OF GOD WORKSHEET	119
SMALL GROUP LEADER'S GUIDE	121
APPENDIX A: HOW TO READ THE BIBLE	123
APPENDIX B: HOW TO MEMORIZE SCRIPTURE	125
APPENDIX C: HOW TO PRAY	127
APPENDIX D: HOW TO BECOME A CHRISTIAN	129

INTRODUCTION

Have you ever received a phone call that stops your heart?

About five years ago, I received a phone call in the middle of the night from my then teenage daughter. She was in a car accident and was stranded. Our conversation was punctuated with many "clicks." In her adrenaline haze, she would call to get an answer to a question and then hang up. My momma's heart kept racing every time she called. I tried to slow my heart by deep breathing and lying in bed, but my mind raced over all the terrible scenarios I could imagine. *Was she hurt? Who was with her? Where was she? How could I get to her?*

After her third call in as many minutes, my husband, Dave, woke up. She called again before I could tell him what little I knew. She told me, finally, that she was not hurt and she was not alone. Both of these facts allowed me to breathe a little slower. She hung up quickly again as Dave jumped out of bed to get dressed. We lived about six hours from where she attended college, yet as her daddy, he was getting ready to go on a mission to rescue her. I quickly told him what little I knew. She was not hurt or alone but had been in a car accident.

When she called again, she was on the brink of losing it. We called it "going over the edge." I spoke sharply to her, "Rachel, breathe with me! Take a deep breath in, hold it, one, two, three. Release it slowly. Breathe in again, hold it, one two three, release." Her panic slowed, she started breathing better, and she stepped back from the edge. Dave sat down and grabbed my hand. She told us she was in Buffalo, she hit another car and was with a group of friends. One of her friends had family that lived nearby so they all would stay there until morning. My heart rate slowed a little. Then click, and my panic reemerged. I turned towards Dave and we started to pray.

Six years before this accident, God in His wisdom gave me a mission to study His names or Call Signs. Every time my daughter hung up on me, I turned to God in prayer. Jehovah-Shalom, The Lord Our Peace, provided me peace between phone calls. I prayed and cried out to Jehovah, The Self-Sufficient One. I called out to Jehovah-Maginnenu, the Lord Our Defense, to protect her and comfort her. Every call from her gave Him the opportunity to remind me of an aspect of His character. He showed me how important it is to know His attributes in my time of need, in my time of rest, in my everyday life, and especially as a parent of teens and young adults.

Communication with God comes through prayer. Jesus taught his disciples how to pray and demonstrated this by going away to pray often. As believers, we have the privilege of calling on Him by name. And there is a name that provides for every need, solves every problem, wins every battle, and comforts every pain. This realization inspired this book. The more we know God, the more powerful and effective our prayers become.

* * *

The more we know God, the more powerful and effective our prayers become.
* * *

Do you remember the movie *Top Gun*? Tom Cruise's fellow aviators call him "Maverick" and his co-pilot "Goose." These names are military Call Signs. The concept is similar to when children choose nicknames for each other. In the military, you don't get to choose your own call sign; the people who know you best decide for you. It becomes your nickname and communicates different attributes about you.

Military members use Call Signs to designate their position, area of responsibility, and authority. In the heat of battle, it is critical to know who you are calling and why. You wouldn't call a personnel specialist when you need an airstrike or an intelligence analyst when you need a medic. It is essential to trust the person you call can meet your needs.

Each military member has a specific mission within the military. The seed God placed in my heart to learn about His names over eleven years ago grew into a mission. My mission was to write about the names of God and tell the people around me about Him, to share His attributes and how they impact our lives, prayers, and missions. Jesus gave us the Great Commission in Matthew 28:16-20. He also gives us our own personal mission. Your mission will be different from mine and change over time. The more I learned about God, the more prepared I became for my mission. With the preparation also came attacks, setbacks, discouragement, and excitement. In every challenge I face, God proves He is capable of meeting my every need.

Delving into some of the names people in the Bible used to call on God led me to a greater understanding of His attributes and empowered my prayer life. God has many names, which people call God after learning about His attributes. We will study one of the names God gave himself, Jehovah. Each name shows an attribute, a part of the character of God. In many Old and New Testament stories, we will discover Jehovah-Maginnenu, The Lord Our Defense. From Genesis to Revelation, Jehovah-Maginnenu defends His faithful believers; He is never surprised by what happens. Even in today's uncertain times, with military deployments and civil unrest, Jehovah sees each of us and is with us. Jehovah's name reminds us that He never changes; He is the great I AM. Just as He loved and watched over the Israelites in Egypt and the desert, He watches over us and loves us today. Many times, our circumstances make us feel alone—deployments, the heartache of miscarriage, loss of family members—but Jehovah-Raah, the Lord Our Shepherd, is waiting to hold us as we cry out to Him.

This book covers six names for God that speak to the challenges all women face in every stage of life. However, as my original and overwhelming research proves, there are many more names for God in the Bible. This study is designed to help you identify other names in Scripture and give you the confidence to pray those attributes back to God. After studying the names of God, you will be empowered to accomplish God's Mission.

God doesn't change; we simply experience different facets of His character. He has so many names because He has so many attributes. Some attributes are descriptive like, Exalted One or God of Sight. God reveals some names to people, such as the Lord Our Provider, Healer, Shepherd, or Peace. God has several names, which He calls Himself. Creator, Self-Existent One, All-Sufficient One, and Lord and Master are the Call Signs He used to help people understand who He is. Knowing His character is critical because it gives us the confidence to know when we call out, He will answer.

He Is Jehovah! is my second book about God's Names or Call Signs. You don't have to complete the first one: "*Call Signs: How Knowing God's Character Empowers Women to Accomplish His Mission,*" to work on this one. All of the names help women grow in their understanding of the attributes of God.

He Is Jehovah is a Bible study that helps women grow in their understanding of God's attributes. The goal is to empower you to share about God's promises wherever He places you. We will study one name each week for six weeks. You can do the study on your own or in a small group setting. Each name concludes with a prayer to start your conversation with God and some discussion questions to help you see how to apply God's character to your life.

As a fellow daughter of Jehovah, the Self-Sufficient One, I have prayed that Jehovah-Jireh (The Lord Our Provider) would minister to your every need as you discover ways to connect with Jehovah-Shalom (The Lord Our Peace) more deeply through His Word, worship, and prayer.

Jennifer

1. JEHOVAH: SELF-SUFFICIENT ONE

God said to Moses, "I AM WHO I AM." And he said, "Say this to the people of Israel: 'I AM has sent me to you.' Exodus 3:14

Jehovah is the eternal, unchanging, self-existent, covenant-keeping God. He is, He was, and He will always be God. He is the all-loving, all-knowing, sinless God. Yahweh is the Hebrew word for God. It is such a powerful name that it is not written out, instead, it is written YHWH. Yahweh was changed to Jehovah in Latin. Mankind may change how they write His name, yet Jehovah does not change.

Women are not known for sitting around and doing nothing. Even when I watch movies, I usually knit or do something with my hands. One of my favorite movies is *Pride and Prejudice*. In one scene, several characters discuss what an "accomplished" woman must be able to do. Listening to everything a woman must do sounds impossible for a whole group of women, much less one woman. However, most women are in constant motion and working on their mission.

It is not easy for me to sit and wait, which is why I needed weeks to sit with God, waiting to heal. Breaking my leg in three places and dislocating my ankle were two competing injuries. For a dislocation, the doctor told me they would want me to get into physical therapy quickly to strengthen the tendons and reduce swelling. Unfortunately, that is the exact opposite of healing from a broken bone, let alone three breaks. He gave me the choice to heal the bone correctly and know that my ankle would swell or do ankle strengthening and risk major bone problems. I chose the bones and worked hard on keeping my ankle up so the swelling would not be too huge. Sitting, waiting, and elevating my ankle made my days drag on. Yet that is when God revealed the name, Jehovah, which means Self-Sufficient One.

I want to be up and moving, growing, changing. Most people are like me, we like to grow. God created us that way. We are always growing: physically, mentally, or spiritually. Sometimes growth is good, and other times we change in ways that are not good. Our growth can help us with our mission or divert our focus from it.

Spiritual growth has been a constant struggle, but that does not mean I have continually grown closer to God. I can say I was growing closer to God many times in my life, but there are also plenty of instances of moving in the opposite direction. Other times I would not say I was growing away from God, instead, **I was simply not watching where I was growing spiritually.** When I was in college, one of my friends talked about going to church, and he quoted many scriptures. Yet he called God the "life force of the world." I started using the pronoun "it" for God. One of my Christian friends heard me and asked me what I was saying. She talked with me for hours about Jehovah, the Self-Sufficient One. God is not Allah, He is not mother nature, nor "a life force." He named Himself "I AM who I AM." Nothing created God; nothing can destroy God. The world will pass away, but God will not.

***

**Nothing created God, nothing can destroy God.
The world will pass away, but God will not.**
***

I feel like I am the nation of Israel in the Old Testament. I think I am growing towards God, but then I look and realize I have been growing away from Him.

When the Israelites were in the desert, God led them with a pillar, yet they grumbled and complained. They had a huge manifestation of God's direction, an actual path yet they still wanted to turn away from His path. I often want God to give me visible signs, as the Israelites had to show me which path to take. He uses the Holy Spirit to show me people and ideas on the right path, but I must listen and choose.

His path is perfect, just like He is perfect. Jehovah means "The Self-Sufficient One." Jehovah stands for "I AM WHO I AM." God is God. He always has been and always will be. He does not change. He is the Alpha and the Omega. He is the same in the beginning as He will be in the end. He is the same in all books of the Bible. He is love, and His love never changes. People may fail us, and time will age us, but God doesn't change.

This Name of God was hard for me. When I first started looking into it, I thought that I could handle Jehovah. I thought it was "just" His Name, but looking more closely revealed more and more to me. He does not change, no matter what I do, no matter how I grow, no matter what happens. He will be Jehovah.

I used to think God changed, that He grew as I grew. Now, I realize that Jehovah, "I AM WHO I AM," does not change. Although He doesn't change, He wants me to change. His mission for my life is always to share His love, both around me and across the world. His great commission is to tell everyone that He is Jehovah, the God of Love.

He is Jehovah. He is constantly providing for us, healing us, leading us, and breathing His life into us.

"I AM WHO I AM" reminds us that He was never created. Nothing is greater than Jehovah. Nothing created Him, He created everything. He will never be destroyed. This was shown to us by Christ's death on the cross. He died in His human body, but He was not destroyed. He rose again and is alive with God. He is the same God before the resurrection as after but now we can live with Him. He did not change, His death allowed us to be redeemed, made pure, washed cleaned. "I AM WHO I AM" wants us to become more like Him.

Becoming more like Jehovah sometimes means turning away from the way we always do things. I am rather like Moses. When God gave him a mission, Moses had excuses. I have lots of excuses for why I don't spend time learning about God—too busy, too tired, and don't know how to study the Bible. The list is long. I need to stop the excuses and start becoming more like Jehovah. For me that included sitting and pondering God's Word more. Sitting, learning to be patient, thoughtful, and peaceful.

Photo by Andy Watkins on Unsplash

God called himself Jehovah in the story of the burning bush found in Exodus 3:1-4:17. Moses experienced Jehovah very personally when Jehovah spoke to Moses out of the burning bush and told him his mission–where to go and what to do. Oh, how I long for that clear communication. But if I look at my past even if Jehovah spoke clearly to me, I probably would talk back like Moses did. I think we are all rebellious and want to choose our own way. If you doubt this, look at a two-year-old. When told to go one way, most two-years-old will stomp defiantly in another direction. I am often like that child.

Another person who met Jehovah was Jonah. Jonah was a prophet whom Jehovah told to go to Nineveh. Jonah turned from God and tried to go to Tarshish thinking he could hide from Jehovah and avoid the mission God had for him to accomplish. Instead, God knew where Jonah was the whole time. Even in the deepest part of a ship or in the belly of a great fish, God knew.

Jonah 1:17 says, "And the LORD appointed a great fish to swallow up Jonah. And Jonah was in the belly of the fish for three days and three nights." Jehovah gave Jonah a divinely issued "time-out" by having Jonah spend three days in the belly of a great fish. (One pastor I listened to mentioned that he was in the fish for three days like Jesus was in the tomb for three days.) How many times do I need a time-out to stop and obey God? Yes, I am still a two-year-old.

This divinely issued "time-out" allowed Jonah to reflect and ponder about God and God's mission for him. God's "time-out" is always best but sometimes it is hard to accept. We all need time to ponder God. It just depends on how open we are to learning. One of my divinely issued "time-outs" was six weeks on bed rest to recover from my broken leg. Some have been short, others longer depending on how willing I am to listen.

I am sure being swallowed by a great fish is far grosser than I can ever imagine. I do not like even putting worms on hooks to catch fish, let alone putting my hand in a fish to pull out the hook. However, Jehovah uses many different means to get us to remember who He is. "Time-outs" can be chosen by us or sent by God.

I often choose "time-outs." I will spend a day fasting and praying. He will meet me in my "time-out." It can be a sweet time, or it can be a struggle to focus and listen. Fasting helps me embrace peace and clarity. Jehovah is not different when I fast, instead, I am different because I surrender my "busy-ness" into His presence and just spend time with Him. Sometimes we don't choose our "time-outs," God does.

Looking back over the time God moved us from Germany to Fort Irwin California, I realized He had sent me to a desert physically, literally in the middle of nowhere. Yet this place was an oasis with abundant spiritual refreshment. My time in the "desert" prepared me for my time in South Carolina. I look at my time in South Carolina as a "time-out."

He moved me to a home, not on a military base. It was the first time in 11 years on active duty that we lived off-post. I had to work harder to make friends. I had friends, but I felt very isolated and different from my neighbors. My friends were not next door or down the street like on military bases. The friends I made in South Carolina are wonderful women I value to this day. It was simply harder to meet and make friends, but this caused me to spend more time by myself and with God. Jehovah does not change, He changes people.

* * *

Jehovah does not change, He changes people.
* * *

Jonah needed a more orchestrated "time-out." God allowed a large fish to swallow him, in order to keep him alive yet to stop him from running from Jehovah. I needed a drastic pause to force me to stop running from God, which happened when my leg was broken.

I had been studying the practice of fasting to teach a workshop about it. But in the back of my mind, I was worrying about the future. I did not even realize the worry was back there many times. Jehovah put me in a "time-out," so He could meet with me. Jonah needed three days, being a slow learner, or just very stubborn, I needed more than six weeks.

Jehovah showed me how my worry affected our time together. I would spend time with Jehovah but not share my worries with Him. If I did voice them, I did not turn them over to Him. I kept worrying and fixating on the things I could not change or did not know.

After being in the big fish, Jonah turns back to God:

> *"The waters closed in over me to take my life;*
> *the deep surrounded me;*
> *weeds were wrapped about my head*
> *at the roots of the mountains.*
> *I went down to the land*
> *whose bars closed upon me forever;*
> *yet you brought up my life from the pit,*
> *O Lord (Jehovah) my God.*
> *When my life was fainting away,*
> *I remembered the Lord,*
> *and my prayer came to you,*
> *into your holy temple.*
> *Those who pay regard to vain idols*

> *forsake their hope of steadfast love,*
> *But I with the voice of thanksgiving*
> *will sacrifice to you;*
> *what I have vowed I will pay.*
> *Salvation belongs to the Lord!"*
> Jonah 2:6-9

Jonah was thankful he had come to this place. He offered his life as a living sacrifice to God. Jehovah did not change, instead, He helped Jonah change by placing him in a "time-out." God told Jonah to, "Arise, go to Nineveh that great city, and call out against it." (Jonah 1:2a and 3:2a) He knew what Jehovah wanted him to do, but he did not want to fulfill that mission. After spending time in the big fish, Jonah prays to God and humbles himself. He followed Jehovah's plan. He went to Nineveh where he proclaimed that God wanted to destroy Nineveh. Hearing Jonah's words, the people of the city repented.

Jehovah appears to change in Jonah 3:10 when he proclaims, "When God saw what they did, how they turned from their evil way, God relented of the disaster that he had said he would do to them, and he did not do it." Jehovah does not change, He changes people's hearts.

***

Jehovah does not change, He changes people's hearts.
***

Jehovah always wants people to repent and turn back to Him. We see this again and again with the Israelites all through the Old Testament. He loves people. He wants them to turn to Him, even today, even on the last day of time. He wants us to live with Him in heaven. That does not change. Yet, He is perfect and righteous, so He cannot have evil with Him. He cannot allow evil to dwell with Him. Through Jesus, He has brought us out of death and sin.

That is why He sent Jonah to Nineveh to bring His message of love and hope to the people there. He wanted them to repent and turn back to Him. Jonah brought the message but his heart was not like God's heart. Jonah did not understand God's commission and wanted the people of Nineveh to be destroyed even after they changed. Jonah blamed the people of Nineveh for making him come there and for his time in the fish. He did not want to forgive them. He did not embrace God's mission in his life.

Have there been times in your life when God's plan doesn't make sense? There have been many times when God's plan left me scratching my head in dismay. I have often wondered, "What is going on?" Jonah must have felt this way. God told Jonah what was going to happen to Nineveh if they did not change. Yet they did change after learning about Jehovah's love, and they stopped doing the things that angered God. They returned to God's path. God did change–He did what he always does with repentant sinners. He showed the people mercy.

God's Plan is an eternal plan from His eternal perspective. When it does not make sense, I need to trust that my limited and linear perspective may not be able to see things from God's eternal perspective. What percent of the total knowledge of the universe and God's plan do I possess? It is laughable to even consider. Jonah learned from God that he knew nothing of God's plan or His power. Jonah thought he could escape and hide from Jehovah, yet even in the belly of a great fish, Jehovah was with him. Jehovah does not change, He is always with us.

* * *

**Jehovah does not change,
He is always with us.**

* * *

My timelines rarely align perfectly with God's. He will ask me to wait so He can show me a better plan. Sometimes I listen, other times I forge ahead. By forging ahead, I may miss a blessing He had planned or I may cause problems with my mission. God's mission is perfect and I can't mess it up, but I can cause more trials and issues for myself and others. When I wait on God, timing becomes clearer… not necessarily easier. Because I don't wait, He allows trials to come my way.

> *Consider it all joy, my brothers, when you meet trials of various kinds, for you know that the testing of your faith produces steadfastness. And let steadfastness have its full effect, that you may be perfect and complete, lacking in nothing. If any of you lacks wisdom, let him ask God, who gives generously to all without reproach, and it will be given to him. But let him ask in faith, with no doubting, for the one who doubts is like a wave of the sea that is driven and tossed by the wind. For that person must not suppose*

> *that he will receive anything from the Lord; he is a double-minded man, unstable in all his ways.* James 1: 2-8

Jehovah allows trials. He does not change, but He wants us to change, grow, and deepen our love for Him because of the trials. When we face temptation and tribulation, God uses them to grow us in ways that make us more of the person He wants us to be. As Jehovah, the Self-Sufficient One, He cannot change but He desires us to change, to become more like Him. I have learned that when trials come, I need to lean on Jehovah, The Self-Sufficient One.

When God's Plan doesn't make sense, we need to trust that God will finish His story, in the right way and in His perfect time. Trust Jehovah to do His job at just the right time. When I am going through a trial, I often want God to fix it right now. (Cue feet stomping.) Jehovah will bring me through that trial at the right time after I have learned what I need to learn. As a mom, sometimes my trial is not about me learning something. Instead, it may be about my children learning through my trials or their own.

My middle daughter, Dena, has learned patience by watching me battle my temper. I often lose my temper, but I am getting better daily. By working with God and yielding to His plan, I can show Dena that controlling her temper may feel like a never-ending battle but we do make progress. When my son, Andrew, sees me pray for his school and sacrifice for his education, he internalizes the idea that learning is important. I want them each to learn these valuable lessons, but it will be in God's time.

No matter where we are in life, I try to remember God sees our whole life within His "Big Picture." Sometimes I think what I do in private does not matter in the big picture. But if I am procrastinating and making people wait then I am causing problems for them. If I do not do what God has given me as a mission to do, then others have to pick up what I do not do. My mission failures impact others.

As a military wife, I often wonder about God's plan. Why did we move to Fort Irwin, the Pentagon, or Germany? At the time of each move, I did not understand God's plan. Looking back, I can see so many people I met through my time in each place who have changed my life. One planted the seed to teach at workshops, one taught me how to fast, others showed me what true friendship looks like, and one counseled me about how always focusing on the negative can ruin your outlook on life. Each friend had something to teach me and by living life together, I learned far more than I would have on my own.

When God's plan does not make sense, I have learned to trust that His grace and love apply to all people. Jehovah loved the people of Nineveh just like He loved Jonah. God taught Jonah about compassion.

> *But God said to Jonah, "Do you do well to be angry for the plant?" And he said, "Yes I do well to be angry, angry enough to die." And the Lord said, "You pity the plant, for which you did not labor, nor did you make it grow, which came into being in a night and perished in a night. And should not I pity Nineveh, that great city, in which there are 120,000 persons who do not know their right hand from their left, and also much cattle?"*
> Jonah 4:9-11

God's Plan did not make sense to Jonah, but Jonah learned the same lesson God is teaching me—that God's grace and love apply to ALL people. Jehovah does not want anyone to perish. The Great Commission Jesus gives us is to tell the world about His love. He wants all to come to Him for salvation. In the New Testament, we learn about that in John 3.

> *"For God so loved the world that he sent his one and only Son that whoever believes in him should not perish, but have eternal life. For God did not send his Son into the world to judge the world, but in order that the world might be saved through him."* John 3:16-17

Jesus saved, still saves, and will continue to save. Jehovah does not change His desire for everyone to come to Him. He wants us to turn towards Him and be saved. His main mission for every believer is to share the Gospel with those around us.

2 Peter 3:9 states, "The Lord is not slow about His promise, as some count slowness, but is patient toward you, not wishing for any to perish but for all to come to repentance." This coincides with Jonah. Jehovah does not want anyone to perish and will save all who repent. Jonah learned that God's time is not his time. God's Plan will often not coincide with our timing. Many times, we will wait, and He will act. Other times, He calls us to act, and then, through our obedience, He will act.

We are to become more like God. **Jehovah is love**. Jehovah is unchanging, never-ending love. We must become more like Him by being more loving. So many wars and problems have come from intolerance and the lack of love. Hebrews 13:8 says, "Jesus Christ is the same yesterday and today and forever." Because He does not change, we must change to become more like Him.

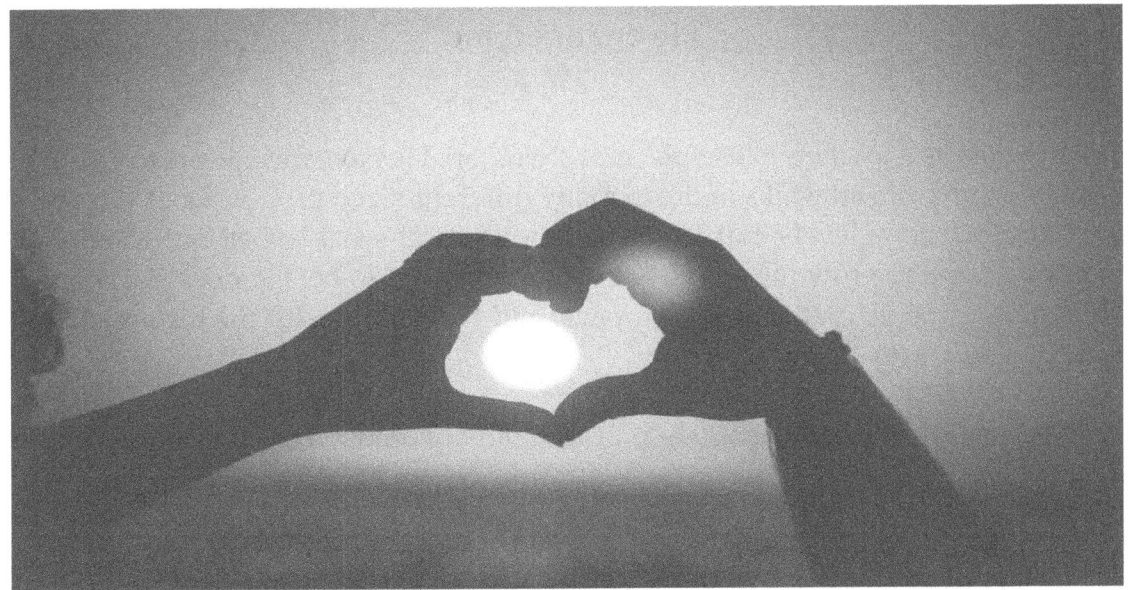

Photo by Mayur Gala on Unsplash

* * *

Jehovah is unchanging, never-ending love.

* * *

He loves us in spite of our sins. We need to love everyone but not their sins. We need to love ourselves and rid ourselves of our sins. The Holy Spirit convicts our hearts of their sinfulness and empowers us to overcome that sin and become more like God. While I was sitting, waiting to heal, God was able to change my heart. I am a teacher, yet I had forgotten my love of teaching. I taught chemistry and physics for eleven years in public schools. I love teaching about science, finance, kids, dogs, whatever.

He called me gently to study Him on my own. Studying His Word without a guide led me to many different scriptures daily. He drew me into His Word and showed me connections to the everyday world I had been missing. He drew me into a great period of discovery. Previously I used books to guide me through my study. He called me to learn about Him personally. Jehovah did not change, He changed me.

* * *

Jehovah did not change, He changed me.

* * *

He grew me as a teacher, a disciple, and a woman. He gave me a heart to teach, to teach women from all walks of life in many different-sized groups. Does this scare me? Yes, on many levels, but I look to Jehovah and see The Self-Sufficient One waiting for me to grow into the woman He wants me to be. He does not change, He will love me no matter what happens, and He will be with me through every time of study, prayer, and teaching.

As I prepared to teach a workshop at a regional conference, He brought me to Romans.

> *For by the grace given to me I say to everyone among you not to think of himself more highly than he ought to think, but to think with sober judgment, each according to the measure of faith that God has assigned. For as in one body we have members, and the members do not all have the same function, so we, though many, are one body in Christ, and individually members one of another. Having gifts that differ according to the grace given to us, let us use them: if prophecy, in proportion to our faith; if service, in our serving; the one who teaches, in his teaching; the one who exhorts, in his exhortation; the one who contributes, in generosity; the one who leads, with zeal; the one who does acts of mercy, with cheerfulness.*
> Romans 12: 3-8

Jehovah has changed the way I think about teaching. I used to think I was the one doing the teaching, but now I know God is the one doing the teaching through me.

"I know the plans I have for you," declares the LORD (Jehovah), "plans for welfare and not for evil, to give you a future and a hope." (Jeremiah 29:11). As He gave me that verse, He also took me to the verses that follow: "Then you will call upon me and come and pray to me, and I will hear you. You will seek me and find me when you seek me with all your heart." (Jeremiah 29:12-13) I often quote verse 11, but He focused me on verses 12 and 13.

I need to call upon Jehovah, to come and pray to Him. He will listen. I need to seek Him and He will let me find Him *when* I search with all my heart. Searching with all my heart is a huge job. Things of this world crowd out time with God. These things are not necessarily all bad in and of themselves. But when they get in the way of time with God, they become things that hinder us. I think of Jesus who needed time away from ministry to pray. Luke 5:16 says, "But he (Jesus) would withdraw to desolate places and pray." I need to take time to be with Jehovah. God took Jonah away for some time to turn back to Him and He gave me a divine time out to seek Him for myself.

If we search after Jehovah, we become more like the amazing "I AM WHO I AM." God doesn't change. He wants us to change because His plan is for us to prosper eternally. I know that my plans are full of holes, things I and others fail to do. I can get distracted and forget important facts, events, and assignments, but God's mission to share His love with others is the most important thing I will ever do. Even though I don't always feel equipped to handle the challenges I face, God is faithful to empower me by His grace and love to fulfill His commission. That often requires me to exchange my plans for His.

Yet, Jehovah doesn't change; He is still the eternal, unchanging, self-existent, covenant-keeping God. Because He doesn't change, we can trust Him in every situation we face. Knowing this about Him increases our intimacy with Him because we can expect Him to always act in accordance with His character. Even when His plan surprises us, we can trust that it is for our good. We serve and worship the powerful, all-knowing Jehovah. He empowers us to serve Him and praise Him. This name covers so many characteristics of God. He revealed different facets of his power to people at specific times. By His great love and grace, He provides all we need to do what He asks of us, which leads us to Jehovah-Jireh, Our Provider. But before we move on to the next chapter, let's spend some time in prayer and discussion about Jehovah.

Prayers to Jehovah

Jehovah, You never change. You don't change when the sun is shining. You don't change when it is raining. You are the same in storms or in good times. You never change.

Jehovah, You are worthy of praise. Nothing compares to You. You are eternal. You have no beginning and no end. You have always been. You never change.

Your love is overwhelming. It flows over us, heals our hearts, lifts us up, draws us together, and never changes.

Your Word has always been. It saves us, transforms our hearts, corrects us, rebukes us, trains us, and encourages us. Your Word never changes.

Jehovah is the same yesterday, today, and tomorrow. You don't change with politics, popular opinions, or cultural norms. You don't change with time. You are the same. You never change.

My feelings change. My emotions change. You, Jehovah, do not change. You always love. You always want the best for me and my family. You always want us with You. Jehovah, You do not change.

During times of moving, You are with me. During times of change, You are with me. When kids go off to school, You are with me. Thank you for comforting me, Jehovah.

When people leave me, You remain by my side. When I cry out in the night because I am alone, You hear me and comfort me. You never change. You don't leave me. Thank you.

When my family members despair, Jehovah, You are there. When my spouse is far away, Your love reminds me that I am loved. Your love comforts those whose wounds I can't see. Your love comforts those who are lost.

Thank You for never changing, Jehovah.

Amen.

Questions for Discussion

God said to Moses, "I AM WHO I AM." And he said, "Say this to the people of Israel: 'I AM has sent me to you.' Exodus 3:14

These questions can be used for personal study or group discussion.

1. Look back over your life and tell a story about a time when you saw God's plan unfold in your life. Does that story remind you of any Bible stories of God's faithfulness?

2. How has God shown you His mission for you at your current duty station or current stage of life?

3. Where are you fighting against God's mission in your life?

4. How have you seen God working in other people's lives?

5. When Jehovah's plan doesn't make sense, what can you do?

6. Jehovah never changes. How have you seen His immutable character despite your changing circumstances?

7. What verses can you use to show that Jehovah doesn't change?

8. In the Bible, we are told to praise Jehovah. Find at least three verses that talk about praising Jehovah.

9. How will your increased understanding of God as Jehovah, empower your prayer life? Write out a prayer to Jehovah claiming the promises and character of God indicated by this Call Sign.

Notes:

2. JEHOVAH-JIREH: THE LORD OUR PROVIDER

Photo by Tom Bradley on Unsplash

So Abraham called the name of that place, "The LORD will provide"; as it is said to this day, "On the mount of the LORD it shall be provided." **Genesis 22: 14**

It's our natural, human tendency to focus on what we lack—maybe a job, finances, a spouse, friends, an easy life, health, or a child. Although Jehovah-Jireh is my Provider, I am still learning His plan and His timing are rarely my plan or my timing.

The Lord Our Provider was the name God impressed on my heart in the days leading up to my ankle surgery. He showed me many ways He provided for me as well as stories of His provision in the Bible.

The morning of my surgery dawned bright and clear which encouraged me. The doctor inserted four screws in my leg to put it back together, and the surgery went well. Afterwards, I was not allowed to put any weight on my leg for six to eight weeks, but God provided for me in countless ways. Some of them were little and some were huge but all were amazing. That was when I started to see how God's names show us different facets of His character. Jehovah-Jireh, my Provider, had been working in my life before, but this was when I really noticed Him.

The first provision was for my kids. He knows right where to reach a mama's heart. At the time, our kids were fifteen, ten and a half, and nine. People called to tell me they would be happy to drive my kids to school.

Jehovah-Jireh provided people I trusted to help with my children which reminded me of Isaac and Abraham. God provided Abraham with a son late in life, then told Abraham to sacrifice him. Abraham was willing to trust God and obey, even in the face of an impossible situation. In Genesis 22:1-24, God provided a lamb, a ram actually, for the sacrifice in replacement of Isaac. Much like Abraham had to follow God and obey, I had to first follow God.

I accepted Christ as my Savior when I was a teenager, but it took many years for me to learn about Him through Bible study and prayer. In fact, I'm constantly learning. In my immobilized state, He provided me with people to take care of my children. I learned to trust and obey Him when He told me to allow others to take care of my kids. We all know how hard it is to accept help.

Perhaps my favorite thing God provided was food. Oh, I wish I could describe the wonderful meals ladies provided. It was diverse, plentiful, and delicious. God wanted to make sure I learned this lesson about provision. He made it so bountiful I had to call people and ask them not to bring any more food so we could eat leftovers and clear out my refrigerator. Talk about humbling. Asking them to tap the brakes on the meal train reminded me how amazingly blessed I was. The meals did not last just one or two weeks, they lasted the full six weeks of my recovery. In fact, I had to tell them to stop blessing us when it was time to move out of our house.

My last day of Bible study at Protestant Women Of the Chapel (PWOC) was the day before we left Fort Jackson. Jehovah-Jireh had a grin on His face that day. As I was about to share and thank the ladies for blessing my socks off, six more ladies came to apologize because they didn't get a chance to bring me food and to ask forgiveness for not being good friends. My jaw hit the floor, I thought I was blessed beyond measure yet these ladies were apologizing for not being a part of the blessing. God burdened their hearts to confess while I was thinking I was over-blessed. The Lord Our Provider knows all your needs and provides abundantly.

* * *
The Lord Our Provider knows all your needs and provides abundantly.
* * *

When I think back to the early years of our youngest daughter, Dena's life, I can see how abundantly God blessed me despite difficult circumstances. Out of her first sixty months, Dave was home ten. People asked me how I handled life with three kids under nine and I repeatedly claimed, "I did not handle it."

My patience wore as thin as a toddler's favorite blanket. I continually fell apart at night and sometimes during the day. A glass of spilled milk could cause me to scream at my children or burst into tears. Many days they would look at me with confusion and pain. Eventually, I would get myself together to continue my mothering mission until bedtime. I remember sitting outside a child's bedroom, each one at a different time, sobbing over how bad a mother I was. After my deep sobbing, I would fall asleep exhausted. In the morning, God provided me with more grace than I could have imagined. Each day my children would wake up and start their day, still loving me, no matter how much I thought I had failed them. No matter how many times I screamed at them, they still loved me. Night after night I crawled under the covers thinking I had failed at being patient, loving, and grace-giving. Yet, every morning God would renew me for another day of learning and growing as a mom to the children He had given me.

One time my mother came to Germany for a two-week visit. Despite being travel-weary, she took one look at me and said, "Leave….I have the kids." She knew I needed some space and time to regroup, but most of all, she recognized my deep need for God during those dark days. And Jehovah-Jireh answered my need by sending her, other family members, and even my husband to me, at just the right time to ease the burden so I could lean into Him.

During a thirteen-month deployment, Dave asked when I wanted him to come home for his two-week break mid-tour. Instantly I replied, "Around Halloween." My mother and my in-laws flew to Germany a couple of times a year to see their grandkids (and me too, I think). They all enjoyed visiting during Thanksgiving,

Christmas, or even summer when it was beautiful in Germany. No one was likely to visit at the end of October, but I knew my kids would be thrilled to show their daddy off to everyone while Trick-Or-Treating. I still remember their proud faces as they bounded back toward our home where I sat to hand out candy. It was wonderful. We also went to the German mountains, saw the beautiful leaves, and drank hot chocolate. Jehovah-Jireh made it a perfect time to rest and recuperate.

Each and every day of Dave's deployments was long, but whether it was seven months or thirteen, it passed quickly. Most of the time, I clung to God daily and allowed Him to deal with the passing of time, but on the days when I focused on the days left in the deployment I would cry out to God in desperation. His mission for me to be a military wife and mother seemed overwhelming. Then, He would gently remind me that He was (and always will be) with me. Jehovah-Jireh provided above and beyond what I needed to deal with each deployment (four in five years). Now, when I wonder if I could survive another deployment, temporary assignment, military move, or any other challenging life circumstance, the verses from Ephesians 3 come back to me. He will give me **more** than I ask or think. He knows what I need and when I need it. I often want things before I need them, but He knows the perfect time to provide things, like patience, writing skills, or a visit from my husband.

> *"Now to Him who is able to do far more abundantly than all that we ask or think, according to the power that works within us, to him be the glory in the church and in Christ Jesus to all generations forever and ever. Amen."*
> Ephesians 3:20-21

Think over those verses. Our Jehovah-Jireh is able to do more than we can ask or even think. He is always working. He desires to work more and more in our hearts, our minds, all areas of our lives. His power works in us, providing us with all that we need and more than we know. God is preparing us to do the work, the mission, He wants us to do. When the time comes for us to do that work, He will provide us with what we need.

* * *

**When the time comes for us to do His work,
He will provide us with what we need.**

* * *

His name, Jehovah-Jireh, "The Lord Provides," reminds me that He will provide and He has provided in so many creative and different ways. Sometimes I think He wants to bless me with more patience, grace, love, yet I am not ready. I am extremely independent, so I love to do things on my own or in my own strength. During deployments, I would often forget to spend time with God. My mornings were full of children and my evenings were full of my self-pity. Instead of seeing how Jehovah-Jireh provided, I focused on myself.

Looking back now I see how He blessed me beyond measure. I do wonder if I had spent more time with Him would I have received more blessings? I insist on doing things my way, in my strength, and in my timing. My own strong will and extreme independence often limit me in many ways. I think selfishly and short-term, while God thinks globally and eternally. He wants to use me to change the world when I feel like I can't even change one more diaper, do one more load of laundry, or make one more meal. When I am feeling overwhelmed by my sliver of the world, the story of Elijah and the widow comes to mind.

Photo by Roberta Sorge on Unsplash

Take a few minutes to read 1 Kings 17:8-24.

It is a good story about Elijah, a prophet of God who met a widow as she was literally running out of food. She was preparing the last meal for her son and herself when Elijah arrived and asked her to make a meal for him. Look at 1 Kings 17:14-16. How did Jehovah-Jireh provide for the widow?

God supplied them with oil and grain beyond what was in their jar. He used Elijah mightily to feed them and then also to be present when the son took ill. Many times, God sustained them in multiple ways. God heard Elijah's cry as the prophet's heart broke for the child, and God healed the boy. This healing changed the widow's heart and showed Elijah God's love and power. God encouraged Elijah and reminded him of his mission as a prophet of God.

Abraham was the first to use the name "Jehovah-Jireh." Genesis 22 opens as God tells Abraham to go to Mount Moriah and sacrifice a burnt offering. Read Genesis 22:1-18 for the complete story. How does God furnish the burnt offering? When does he produce it?

I am in awe of Abraham. His faith is truly amazing. If you know his story, you might remember he had prayed for a child for *years*. His wife Sarai is called "barren." She knew the pain of praying month after month for a baby yet receiving her monthly cycle. She and Abram heard the whispers of other women about her infertility. Abram also had to deal with the idea that everything he owned would be passed down to another family after his death.

Like Sarai, my journey to motherhood was not easy. God gave us our oldest, Rachel, but then I miscarried multiple times. By my third miscarriage, the doctors still did not know why. They gave me medicine that allowed me to carry Dena and then Andrew to term. Even in that desolate season where the only thing that felt abundant was loss, Jehovah-Jireh provided me with the right medicine as well as the right doctors to help me. My provider gave me the strength to continue on His mission. He will give you the strength to do His mission.

* * *

**Our provider, Jehovah-Jireh,
gives us the strength to do His mission.**

* * *

In Genesis 13, God promised Abram his descendants would outnumber the dust of the earth, but Abram and his wife Sarai had to wait for their son well past the age when that sort of thing was thought possible. Yet in Genesis 17, Jehovah-Jireh changed Abram's name, meaning "exalted father" to Abraham, meaning "father of nations" and Sarai, meaning "woman of strength", to Sarah, meaning "My woman of strength." God made a promise to them for their future children, He even changed their names to reflect that promise. I am similar to Sarah because I try to figure out God's plan and change His timing. Sarah tried to ease Abraham's desperation with her attempt to out plan God by plotting to get a child through her maid. But that is a story for another name.

Sarah eventually becomes pregnant and gives birth to Isaac. But now, God instructs Abraham to sacrifice that same son. I'm not sure what I would have done in his situation. Would I argue with God or perhaps try to hide? God asked Abraham to follow Him, to be obedient. Once God saw that Abraham was willing to surrender, He provided. Many times, I want God to provide things *now*. Lord, I need direction in my life, *now*. We need money, NOW. God, I need a job, NOW! Lord, save me from this difficult situation, right NOW.

Abraham didn't act like that, though. He followed God's instructions even when he didn't understand or like them. He was willing to give up his future for God and tied up his son. Nowhere do we read what Isaac did or thought, so I wonder what the boy was feeling. Did he see the ram? Was he fighting? Did he trust his dad? Did he trust God?

After the offering was complete, God blessed Abraham. He proclaimed Abraham's offspring would be as many as the stars in the heavens and the sand on the shore. God blessed him after Abraham showed his heart to follow God. Jehovah-Jireh is worthy of our praise.

* * *

Jehovah-Jireh is worthy of our praise.
* * *

I am not good at praising in the midst of troubles. I constantly have to stop and ask God to remind me of one of His names. Many times, He brings Jehovah-Jireh to mind. God is my Provider. He provides me with breath every day, a home, family, pets, health. I may whine that I want more, but He reminds me of what He has already given me, chiefly Jesus. He will often remind me of my mission. We all have different missions that are all part of the Great Commission.

We military women know a good bit about the "ends of the earth" part of spreading the gospel message. As God moves us from one side of the country to the other or farther every couple of years or even sooner, we have the opportunity to see God provide in some very unique ways. Sometimes military spouses ask each other the question: What was your least favorite assignment? I don't like to answer this question, because sometimes the hardest assignment comes with the sweetest friendships. In each place we have lived, God has given me many friends. In Germany, one of my friends had kids the same age, another had older kids, and a third had no kids at all. But each one filled a special area of my life during that season. Even now, many years later, I still love to call and chat with these friends. They are truly a gift from God. Jehovah-Jireh sends me at least one good friend every time we move. We all need at least one person to share good and bad days, the ups, and the downs. God has always known and provided exactly what I needed at every duty station and in every life situation.

In Psalm 91, Jehovah-Jireh reminds me to hold on to Him. He provides for me. I trust in Him and He will rescue me, honor me, and satisfy me. I hold on to Him in love, not selfishly, but because He sent His Son to die for my sins.

> *"Because he holds fast to me in love, I will deliver him;*
> *I will protect him, because he knows my name.*
> *When he calls to me, I will answer him;*
> *I will be with him in trouble; "I will rescue him and honor him.*
> *With long life I will satisfy him*
> *and show him my salvation."* Psalm 91:14-16

These verses talk about long life, yet this is from God's view, not ours. My dad's life was cut short in my way of thinking because my mother lived another 22 years. Yet my dad lived to be 64, which is longer than his sister or several cousins. I am still learning to see God's provisions and to praise Him even in the trials where my struggles cloud His provisions.

King David reminds us of Jehovah-Jireh in Psalm 145. He reminds us to call out to God in our times of need.

> *"The eyes of all look to you,*

> *and you give them their food in due season.*
> *You open your hand;*
> *you satisfy the desire of every living thing.*
> *The Lord is righteous in all his ways*
> *and kind in all his works.*
> *The Lord is near to all who call on him,*
> *to all who call on him in truth."* Psalm 145:15-18

These verses remind us to praise Him for our food. He opens His hand to satisfy our desires. Does this mean He gives us what we want when we ask? No, the next verse reminds us that He is righteous in all His ways and kind in all His works. He is perfect. So when He says, "No," to a desire it means He sees how it will hurt me. Not only that He sees my hurt, but He has already planned and provided a way to make it work out for my good.

Over the years, I have prayed for Him to provide us with more time at a location or a bigger house. He answered both these prayers by sending us back to Fort Leavenworth, Kansas. Our 6,800-square-foot house was part of a historic duplex. It took me a day to clean each of the four levels. He gave me my prayer for a big house. Way beyond what I thought I wanted, to teach me to be satisfied when I'm tempted to question His generosity in other situations.

He also kept us there for three years which is the longest time we've spent in any one location. From this time, I came to realize that staying for so long comes with both good and bad things. We were the people who had to say goodbye to friends who left us, we welcomed new friends just to see them leave before we did. This was challenging for me; I was usually the one who left others. But God taught me to say goodbye which means "God be with you." God taught me to release my friends with this blessing.

Learning about Jehovah-Jireh's desire to grow us and mold us has helped to mature my thinking over the years. When we stop and look around to see what God *has* given us everything changes. Gratitude shifts our focus from what we think we lack to what God has already provided to meet our needs. This understanding of God as Jehovah-Jireh deepens our intimacy with Him by reminding us that we can trust Him to provide for our every need.

Now, when I sense Satan shifting my attention from what God has already provided for me to what I lack, I know I can call on Jehovah-Jireh. As I spent time with my leg elevated, I learned about Jehovah-Jireh. Yet at the same time, I was learning about Jehovah-Jireh, God was showing me a new name, Jehovah-Rapha, my Healer. We'll talk more about Him in the next chapter, but first, let's call on Jehovah-Jireh in prayer and discuss how His provision equips us to accomplish His mission.

Prayer to Jehovah-Jireh

Jehovah-Jireh, The Lord our Provider,
You provide us mercy every day.
Mercy for our sins.
Mercy for our tempers, flaring out of control.
Mercy for our lies, big ones, and little ones.
Mercy for every part of our lives.

Jehovah-Jireh, The Lord our Provider,
You provide us with grace every day.
Grace despite our sins.
Grace for our enemies both foreign and domestic.
Grace for our afflictions, huge diseases, and small scrapes.
Grace for all our adversities, sometimes in our time but always at the right time.

Jehovah-Jireh, The Lord our Provider,
You provide us strength every day.
Strength to overcome sin.
Strength to hold our tongues when we are angry.
Strength to withstand temptations and to restart when we fail.
Strength to wake up every morning even when we want to stay in bed.

Jehovah-Jireh, The Lord our Provider,
You provide us wisdom every day.
Wisdom to overcome sin.
Wisdom to teach our children.
Wisdom to learn more about You.
Wisdom to avoid situations where we could be tempted.

Jehovah-Jireh, The Lord our Provider,
You provide us with a family every day.
Family to help us overcome sin.
Family both close and far.
Family both easy to get along with as well as those that are hard.
A family that loves us and yet may be hard to love.

Amen.

Questions for Discussion

These questions can be used for personal study or for group discussion.

> *So Abraham called the name of that place, "The LORD will provide"; as it is said to this day, "On the mount of the LORD it shall be provided."* **Genesis 22: 14**

1. Here are some of my favorite Old Testament stories. Match the story in the first column with what God provided in the second column.

Ruth & Naomi	Strength to become the foundation of the church
Paul & Silas	Peace and protection during persecution
King David	Faithful companions
Peter	Food and future family

2. What New Testament story shows Jehovah-Jireh granting peace to the new church? (Look in Acts 1-4.)

3. In Judges 6-8, Gideon sees Jehovah-Jireh in many ways. List some of the things God provided.

4. Job had many things taken away from him. Discounting physical things, what did Jehovah-Jireh restore to Job?

5. Read Ezra 6. How did God inspire King Darius to provide for the rebuilding of the temple? How has God provided for you in challenging situations or unusual ways?

6. List some things God brings to your mind about His name Jehovah-Jireh.

7. In what current life situation can you see Jehovah-Jireh at work?

8. How has God provided for you today? How has God provided for you in the past?

9. Where in your life are you asking God to meet a physical, emotional, or spiritual need? What relational needs are you imploring God to heal?

10. How will your increased understanding of God as Jehovah-Jireh, empower your prayer life? Write out a prayer to Jehovah Jireh claiming the promises and character of God indicated by this Call Sign.

Notes:

3. JEHOVAH-RAPHA: THE LORD OUR HEALER

'saying, "If you will diligently listen to the voice of the LORD your God, and do that which is right in his eyes, and give ear to his commandments and keep all his statutes, I will put none of the diseases on you that I put on the Egyptians, for I am the LORD, your healer."' **Exodus 15:26**

As I approach another milestone birthday, each morning I feel more aches and pains. My family members are passing away and my children are flexing their independence, leaving huge holes in my heart. I need healing for these physical and emotional hurts. Jehovah-Rapha means the Lord our Healer. This Name spans so many areas where healing needs to happen.

Healing comes in many forms. Jehovah-Rapha desires to heal us physically, emotionally, and spiritually in His time. This Name was my heart's desire after my accident. I was eager to claim His healing, but Jehovah-Rapha called me to study, ponder, wrestle, and most importantly, allow Him to heal me in His time and His way. I did not want to sit and wait on His time yet sitting is what I did for many weeks.

During my time of physical healing, God allowed my heart to heal from many emotional events I had stuffed deep down inside. My heart's desire was physical healing; His desire was to heal my heart, my body, and my mind of all nature of wounds, some decades old.

When I miscarried my second baby, Timothy, I went right back to work. I believed if I didn't dwell on it then it would not hurt as much. When people asked about my pregnancy, tears would squeeze out no matter how hard I tried to remain brave and strong. I believed if I ignored my pain, and my loss, then I would heal faster. As I tried to shove my pain way down deep, it seemed to leak out at the worst times. When my husband wanted to talk about Timothy, I turned away. Dave was devastated, too, but I did not care because he wasn't the one who had been pregnant. Can you say selfish? Yep, Queen Selfish was my title and I did not even realize it. I stubbornly refused to seek God's healing, because I was mad at Him.

I didn't even care if God wanted to heal this wound. Instead, I shoved it deep down and tried to ignore the pain. My dad passed away shortly after I lost Timothy. Yet another loss I could not handle. I turned further away from God. Anything that could help me, I rejected. Then we lost Grace, and I sank deeper and deeper down into my pain and hurt.

We entered the military shortly after we lost Grace. Jehovah-Rapha sent me friends who understood my pain, but I still wasn't ready to allow Him to heal me. When I found out I was pregnant again, I only told Dave. I did not want anyone else to know; maybe keeping it a secret would prevent my pain. When I started to miscarry Christopher, I just curled up on the floor and prayed for God to stop all this pain. When Rachel, who was only four years old at the time, found me, she raced out to get help. It scared her to see me like that but her actions saved my life. As the lights and sirens of the ambulance cleared the way to the hospital, I vowed to never have any more kids. But God....

Jehovah-Rapha sent me a doctor who figured out why I miscarried. She listened to my story and heard me. She encouraged me to not give up. I stopped my downward spiral, but I did not let go of my pain and hurt. Still, God's Name of Healer was a name I did not know or claim. Jehovah-Rapha, our Healer, endows us with the power to help others.

***
Jehovah-Rapha, our Healer endows us with the power to help others.
***

Dave and I started counseling before Dena was born. Spending time in counseling brought up all the pain of the miscarriages. The pounding blows of losing three kids and my father within a year had shattered my heart into a thousand pieces. Jehovah-Rapha desired to heal me. He wanted to heal me from the emotional pain, as well as the spiritual pain of turning away from Him. Yet, I did not embrace Jehovah-Rapha until God finally broke through to me when my leg injury forced me to sit and heal. Even as I cried out for Him to heal my broken leg, His plan was to restore health to my body, mind, and spirit. He desires to heal us spiritually, mentally, emotionally, and physically.

Photo by Ben White on Unsplash

***
Jehovah-Rapha desires to heal us spiritually, mentally, emotionally, and physically.
***

As I sat, Jehovah-Rapha had my undivided attention. Oh, sure, I tried to avoid Him through TV and computer time but that quickly became boring and made my days drag on. I wanted God to heal my leg and ankle completely. More importantly, I wanted them to heal *quickly*. The sooner I could return to normal activity the better. Yet my unchanging, ever-loving God wanted me to learn about His Name, Jehovah-Rapha. Eventually, I gave up avoiding Him and started learning about all His names.

I jumped into the Word to learn more about the Name, Jehovah-Rapha.

> *I am poured out like water,*
> *and all my bones are out of joint;*
> *my heart is like wax;*
> *it is melted within my breast;*
> *my strength is dried up like a potsherd,*
> *and my tongue sticks to my jaws;*
> *you lay me in the dust of death.*
>
> *For dogs encompass me;*
> *a company of evildoers encircle me;*
> *they have pierced my hands and my feet-*
> *I can count all my bones-*
> *they stare and gloat over me;*
> *they divide my garments among them,*
> *and for my clothing they cast lots.*
>
> *But you, O LORD, do not be far off!*
> *O you my help, come quickly to my aid!*
> Psalm 22:14-19

As I meditated on these scriptures, Jehovah-Rapha drew my attention to verse 18, "They divide my garments among them, and for my clothing they cast lots." Over the years, I have heard this Scripture used to describe Jesus' death. Yet this passage is about our Healer, Jehovah-Rapha. I rescanned the passage, seeing other verses about Jesus' death. Since Jesus is part of the Trinity—God the Father, God the Son, and God the Holy Spirit—it means He is my Healer. He and God are together with the Holy Spirit. When I study God's Word, I often forget about the Trinity. I forget that Jesus is God and He works through the Holy Spirit and the Father.

These verses described me perfectly, I was poured out, defeated, and at the point of despair. While I was looking at these verses, I learned about the Name, Jehovah-Rapha. "But You, O LORD, be not far off; O You, my help, hasten to my assistance," shows my Jehovah-Rapha standing nearby ready to help me. How great is God's Word! Jehovah-Rapha was, is, and will be waiting to heal me, but I must be ready to obey Him. He is ready and waiting to heal us.

* * *

Jehovah-Rapha is ready and waiting to heal us.
* * *

Moses was the first person to claim healing from Jehovah-Rapha. In Exodus, when the Israelites were thirsty, Moses cried out to Elohim to provide water.

> *And he cried to the LORD, and the LORD showed him a log; and he threw it into the water, and the water became sweet.*
> *There the Lord made for them a statute and a rule, and there he tested them, saying, "If you will diligently listen to the voice of the LORD your God, and do that which is right in his eyes, and give ear to his commandments, and keep all his statutes, I will put none of the diseases on you that I put on the Egyptians; for I am the LORD, your healer."*
> *Then they came to Elim, where there were twelve springs of water and seventy palm trees, and they encamped there by the water.*
> Exodus 15:25-27

God healed the Israelites from their thirst after proclaiming some precepts. A precept is a command or principle intended especially as a general rule of action[1]. He gave them four specific things to do:

1. Give earnest heed to the voice of the Lord your God.
2. Do what is right in His sight.
3. Give ear to His Commandments.
4. Keep all His statutes.

---

[1] https://www.merriam-webster.com/dictionary/precept

When I first read this passage, I was struck by the precepts and the "and" which showed up repeatedly. Some people ignore "and," but for me, I see it and wonder if I can do *all* the parts of what God is asking me to do.

* * *
"Give earnest heed to the voice of the Lord your God."
* * *

While many people think this means hearing the voice of God from heaven or through a prophet, it can also mean listening while reading your Bible, during prayers, fasts, or worship at church. This is when God will show you His mission for you.

While my leg was healing, I could not go to chapel with my family. This was challenging because I wanted the sweet time of singing praises to God. Instead, I spent time with my Bible and a notebook. I went through the Psalms and found several psalms which people had put to music. It was wonderful to hear God speak to me through these songs and Psalms. Hearing God's voice does not have to be audible; it can happen when your spirit is at peace and you know God is giving that peace to you. As Christians, we have the privilege of direct access to our Jehovah-Rapha through the peace-giving practice of prayer, night and day.

My daughter, Rachel, once believed I had a "purple phone" that was a direct line to God. When she was little, she watched as I prayed and listened to God's still small voice. She decided I had a direct line to God which she called my "purple phone." When we got orders to move to Texas, I did not use my "purple phone." Instead of paying careful attention to God's direction through prayer and listening, I decided Dave should go to Texas and I would stay in South Carolina until the end of the school year (Rachel's sophomore year). Once my broken leg stopped me, I finally started praying. Once again I jumped to the conclusion, I knew what was best, I believed we should move at the semester mark in mid-January even though Dave had to report on December 1st. Again, after finally stopping to pray, to listen, I heard God's still small voice telling me to move with my husband. We have always believed our family should stay together. God reinforced this to me through a phone call from a school in Texas. If we had moved at the semester mark, Rachel would have lost a whole semester due to conflicting schedules. I knew God wanted us to stay together.

Even if I did have a "purple phone," it would be for God to have my full attention when He talks to me. I often want to have my way, but in moments of deeper clarity, I would rather follow what God wants. I have learned my way is usually the wrong way or at least not the best way. God's plan is always best.

***
"Do what is right in His sight."
***

This one is all-encompassing, we are to do what we know God has said is right. This can mean standing alone sometimes. It means speaking His truth when the world wants us to be politically correct. This can be a lonely thing to do, but how many times throughout history has the Church (universal Church of all believers) stayed silent when we should have been standing up and fighting? It also means doing what is right. I must watch what I do and say. I often avoid conflict, because I want to keep people as friends. God calls us to do what is right in His sight which may not be what others think is right.

When I told my friends at Fort Jackson I could not travel to the conference with my broken leg, they started to plan how they could help me. Their suggestions were well-intentioned, but I knew God had said no to the trip and I needed to listen to Him. If I had gone, I do not know what God would have taught me, but since I did not go I learned to "do what is right in His sight."

***
"Give ear to His commandments."
***

Listen with the intention of obeying and His commandments will guide you. Before I broke my leg, every Sabbath in my house was busy with chapel activities and preparations for the week ahead. As I sat in my bed, the Sabbath became a peaceful time for me. My family would come home from the chapel and often one, two, or all three kids would join me for a movie. They would sit and we would rest. They loved to tell me about all the happenings in the chapel and my son would often recount what songs they sang. That truly blessed my heart. Many times, my Bible reading would match the songs they sang at the chapel. Isn't it just like God to double down on the healing power of His Word and worship?

The term "His commandments" refers to God's law and direction for His people. Five chapters later in Exodus 20:1-17, God formalizes His law by giving Moses the Ten Commandments. My short version is:

1. Have no god before God.
2. Do not make idols or have idols.
3. Do not take the Lord's name in vain.
4. Remember the Sabbath Day.
5. Honor your father and mother.
6. Do not murder.
7. Do not commit adultery.
8. Do not steal.
9. Do not lie.
10. Do not covet your neighbor's things.

These commandments are sometimes overlooked because they are in the Old Testament. People believe Jesus made it so that the Ten Commandments are no longer in force. Jesus told us the reality in Luke 10:27: "And he answered, 'You shall love the Lord your God with all your heart, your soul and with all your strength and with all your mind, and your neighbor as yourself.'" He took the Big Ten and condensed them down into two, all-encompassing commandments. Yet in many ways, I think this is even harder for me to follow. I often find just the phrase, "Love your neighbor as yourself," close to impossible. We always find fault in ourselves as well as others. Loving ourselves can be hard, and loving others even harder.

I know that this is a summary of the commands of God but I am constantly drawn back to the Ten Commandments. Jesus did not break one of these physically, spiritually, or emotionally. He did not even sin in His thoughts. I try to look at the Ten Commandments as Jesus did, from the heart which is very challenging. My mind says one thing and my heart another. Working to become more like Jesus is a daily struggle for me. Lusting after something can make it an idol and if it belongs to somebody else, I'm also coveting. How many times do I look at my bank account and think I need more money to buy more things? How many times do I get angry at my kids? Is that like breaking the commandment not to kill?

What about wanting a newer car or house? I want to have a nice car and a nice house but did I need new ones? God provides us with places to live, which I can turn into homes wherever He sends us. What about bearing false witness? That should be easy to keep, right? Then God reminded me of any number of "little white lies" I tell to avoid hurting people's feelings. Bearing false witness is lying. "Little white lies" are lies nonetheless.

***
The last precept is to "keep all His statutes."
***

Did I want to be healed? Yes. Can I keep all His statutes? Probably not. Statutes are laws He has added to the daily life of His people. Legalism comes from this idea. God gave us freedom in Christ, but we are not to abuse that freedom. Churches and people add on rules to "help" us be better Christians. Some churches frown on wearing jeans to church. Others disapprove when you look too nice on Sunday. For quite a while I wore hats to church. He convicted me that I needed to cover my head in His house. I did this for many years until He lifted this conviction, but in the meantime, it caused lots of conversations about statues and grace. I had several people tell me rules from the Old Testament no longer apply and I tried not to argue. This was something God wanted me to do to honor Him, so I obeyed until He allowed me to stop. He gives us love and grace and we need to serve him out of that love and grace.

In light of these four precepts (Give earnest heed to the voice of the Lord your God, do what is right in His sight, give ear to His commandments, and keep all His statutes), healing was not as easy as I wanted it to be. I had to look at my heart and see where I was in relation to where God wanted me. He wants us to ask for healing.

> *Is anyone among you suffering? Let him pray. Is anyone cheerful? Let him sing praise. Is anyone among you sick? Let him call the elders of the church, and let them pray over him, anointing him with oil in the name of the Lord. And the prayer of faith will save the one who is sick, the Lord will raise him up. And if he has committed sins, he will be forgiven. Therefore, confess your sins to one another and pray for one another, that you may be healed. The prayer of a righteous person has great power as it is working.*
> James 5:13-16

Looking at this passage in light of my broken leg brought me to a new understanding of the power of prayer. God wants us to ask for prayer when we are sick or hurt. He expects us to pray over sick and hurting people. It states, "the prayer of faith will save the one who is sick; the Lord will raise him up."

* * *

Jehovah-Rapha wants us to pray earnestly for those who need healing.

* * *

When my dad was diagnosed with a recurrence of his colon cancer, I was pregnant with my second child, Timothy. I prayed to God to let my dad meet his second grandchild. I thought I was clear that I wanted to witness this meeting. Instead, I miscarried and my dad died less than three months later. God healed my dad up in Heaven and He answered my prayers that my dad might meet his second grandchild and the third, then the fourth.

I did not know how God would answer my prayer, but when they met up in heaven, I was mad. I thought God had broken our agreement. Years later through counseling, prayer, and time, I realized God answered my prayer according to His best plan. My plan would have allowed my dad and my whole family to suffer more and I don't know if I would have my Dena and my Andrew since my three in heaven might have stopped me from having more kids. My plan was for three or four kids. Dave wanted three. God gave us six. Although I still miss my dad daily, I know God's plan allowed me to have a wonderful family. Although my mother is alone, she has spent a wonderful time with her grandchildren and I have grown closer to her through the years.

* * *

Jehovah-Rapha heals in line with His perfect plan.

* * *

There are many people who don't ask for healing because they feel like their situation is not as bad as someone else's. I believe we should ask for healing and work with God toward it, but also understand that healing may not come the way we hope for it. God did not heal Paul from his thorn.

> *So to keep me from becoming conceited because of the surpassing greatness of the revelations, a thorn was given me in the flesh, a messenger of Satan*

to harass me, to keep me from becoming conceited. Three times I pleaded with the Lord about this, that it should leave me. But he said to me, "My grace is sufficient for you, for my power is made perfect in weakness." Therefore I will boast all the more gladly of my weaknesses, so that the power of Christ may rest upon me. For the sake of Christ, then I am content with weaknesses, insults, hardships, persecutions, and calamities. For when I am weak, then I am strong. 2 Corinthians 12:7-10

Sometimes we need "a thorn" to remind us of God's perfect plan. When my ankle aches, I am reminded of my Jehovah-Rapha who has healed me so I can walk and move. God sent us to San Antonio, Texas where Brooks Army Medical Center is located. It is now called SAMMC (San Antonio Military Medical Center). It is a center for wounded warriors and allows family members to join the warrior while he or she receives medical care. Living on an Army base with one of the largest military medical centers taught me not to whine about my ankle. I have sat in waiting rooms with military members who were missing one or more limbs and watched their family members help them get to and from appointments. Some of the families who come there are mad at the military. I have seen some of these families pull together and rely on each other, but I have also seen families break apart due to their warrior's wounds or their own hurts. No matter how Satan twists the situation, I have no doubt that Jehovah-Rapha's desire is to use this place to heal families physically, as well as emotionally and spiritually.

God has blessed me; Jehovah-Rapha healed my leg. Although I did nothing to deserve it, Jehovah-Rapha is constantly healing me physically, emotionally, and spiritually. He has grown me through this pain.

* * *

Jehovah-Rapha wants to heal everyone from the inside out.
* * *

Lost limbs and scars may make us appear broken on the outside, but we can still be whole on the inside. Conversely, we may appear whole and put together on the outside but be broken apart on the inside. Watching these men and women work through injuries both physical and psychological inspired my awe. Many of them remained in the military still fulfilling their mission. Their strength and commitment to their "Battle Buddies" will remind you that no matter what you face, you are never alone. Jehovah-Rapha can help you overcome your wounds and hurts. He can heal you. Sometimes He does it quickly. Other times, He uses time to help us heal.

Almost a year after I broke my leg, I went back to an orthopedic surgeon, because I still had pain in my ankle. He told me he would take out two of my screws. One set of screws had broken, while the other set was still whole.

The night before the surgery, I was not allowed to eat so I prayed during this time of fasting. I prayed to Jehovah-Rapha for peace and healing. I asked to not have any pain from the parts left in, for no more surgeries, and for healing. God reminded me that He was Jehovah-Rapha, my Healer. When the doctor walked in before the surgery, he said, "We are taking out everything. Since we are in there, let's just take out all the hardware so there won't be anything left." I sat there and praised God. He answered my prayers beyond what I could imagine. He knew exactly what I needed before I even knew what I needed. So, I am now hardware-free.

Do I still have pain? Some days I do, but most days I don't notice any physical pain. I know Jehovah-Rapha will be with me. I know He will heal me somehow no matter how this world may break me. Even though I often got frustrated with the pace of my recovery and the length of my healing, I know I learned a great deal from it. Sometimes He heals quickly, but other times He says wait. We may have to wait for healing until we join Him in Heaven, but once we arrive there we will suffer no more. Waiting can be hard, but the more time we spend with Him the more like Him, the more healed and whole, we become.

Jehovah-Rapha wants to heal us from the inside out. He wants us to give up our emotional heartbreaks, our spiritual pain, and our physical wounds. Are you ready to let your Savior heal you? When we call on God as our Jehovah-Rapha, our Healer, He empowers our prayers with requests of emotional, physical, and spiritual healing. We need to release our pain and fear and turn to Jehovah-Raah, The Lord our Shepherd, who is our firm guide and our protector. Before we move on, let's spend a little time praying and discussing our Healer.

Prayer to Jehovah-Rapha

You can pray this prayer for yourself or someone else who needs healing.

Lord, as I pray for healing what I truly desire is You. I pray that You would meet me in my pain. I pray that I turn to You and rely on You.

Pain can help me remember that You are with me. You are with me when I am alone, when I am scared. Thank You for healing my heart, mind, and spirit.

As Paul had a thorn to remind him of Your faithfulness, if You want me to have pain, I pray that I can serve You with this thorn.

If You choose to heal me this side of heaven, I pray that I would give glory to You and speak of Your great mercy. God, please remind me to give You glory every day, every hour, every minute.

Lord, teach me to heed Your voice. Show me areas of my life where I am not listening to You or obeying You. Teach me to hear Your voice even though the world shouts for my attention. Let me fix my eyes on You. Lord, teach me to hear Your voice.

Lord, search my heart. If I have sinned, please show me what I need to repent. Teach me to do what is right in Your sight. If I need to repent and ask forgiveness from someone I've hurt, give me the strength to go to that person. Lord, search my heart.

Lord, if I have ignored any of Your commandments or statutes forgive me. Open my eyes to areas I need to work on. I ask You to write Your commandments and statutes on my heart.

Open my eyes to where I should be serving You. No matter if I have pain or need healing, I can still serve You. Remind me to pray for and encourage others.

Amen.

Questions for Discussion

These questions can be used for personal study or group discussion.

> *'saying, "If you will diligently listen to the voice of the LORD your God, and do that which is right in his eyes, and give ear to his commandments and keep all his statutes, I will put none of the diseases on you that I put on the Egyptians, for I am the LORD, your healer."'* **Exodus 15:26**

1. What does it mean to you to "give earnest heed to the voice of the Lord your God"?

2. How can you "do what is right in His sight" today?

3. Which Commandment do you struggle with most? Why? What areas of your life do you need the Holy Spirit to change?

4. What statutes are you not keeping? Why? How can you change?

5. How has Jehovah-Rapha healed you? What areas still need healing? Look at Matthew 9:20-22. Are there other areas you need healing?

6. Are you willing to wait for healing? Are you willing to rest and wait on God's timing instead of striving to heal without God? Look up Revelation 21:4. How does this verse relate to healing?

7. **Lookup** Matthew 5:17-20. Write it as a prayer to Jehovah-Rapha.

8. What other stories of healing are found in the Bible?

9. If someone dies without being healed, did they lack faith? Why might Jehovah-Rapha let them die? Look up James 5:13-17

10. List all the ways Psalm 147 says Jehovah-Rapha heals.

11. How will your increased understanding of God as Jehovah-Rapha, empower you as you are on your mission? Write out a prayer to Jehovah-Rapha claiming the promises and character of God indicated by this Name.

Notes:

4. JEHOVAH-RAAH: THE LORD OUR SHEPHERD

Photo by Patrick Schneider on Unsplash

"The LORD is my shepherd; I shall not want." Psalm 23:1

Have you ever coached little ones, think three to four-year-olds? I call it "herding cats" as they seem to scatter in every direction, losing interest and focus, distracted by butterflies or dandelions. Herding little kids or cats is truly challenging, but herding sheep can be worse. Jehovah-Raah is the Name of our Shepherd. He works constantly to help me focus on where He wants me to go, protect me safe on my mission, and keep me growing more like Him.

Great Britain hosts sheep herding events. During these trials, shepherds and their dogs have to take a herd of sheep through various tasks, such as moving them from point to point in a meadow, getting them into a run, stopping them, and moving them through a gate. I was fascinated with the sheepdogs who work in tandem with their shepherds. Working together, dogs and shepherds maximize their abilities and the sheep did not stand a chance.

Sheepdogs and shepherds have their own ways of communicating, yet they work as a unit toward the goal of controlling the sheep. God is Triune, He is one God but three equal parts. The Trinity is God the Father, God the Son, and God the Holy Spirit. They are one yet each part has specific jobs and roles. They work in tandem to guide us and show us the path.

As I studied Jehovah-Raah, the Lord Our Shepherd, I turned to Psalm 23.

> *The LORD is my shepherd; I shall not want.*
>
> *He makes me lie down in green pastures.*
> *He leads me beside still waters.*
>
> *He restores my soul.*
> *He leads me in the paths of righteousness for his name's sake.*
>
> *Even though I walk through the valley of the shadow of death,*
> *I will fear no evil, for you are with me; your rod and your staff, they comfort me.*
>
> *You prepare a table before me in the presence of my enemies.*
> *you anoint my head with oil; my cup overflows.*
>
> *Surely goodness and mercy shall follow me all the days of my life,*
> *and I will dwell in the house of the LORD forever.*
> Psalm 23: 1-6

As I meditated on this Psalm, I remembered the sheep herding trials. My sisters and I laughed so hard at the sheep because they did not seem to know where to go or what to do. We were mesmerized by the dogs and the way the shepherds controlled them. While domestic sheep may act similar to "wild sheep," they look very different. Both male and female "wild sheep" have horns, but domestic sheep are bred without them. The hair (wool) on domestic sheep is longer than "wild sheep." Wild sheep had long coarse hair with a short downy undercoat, which under domestication gradually became wool, while the long hair disappeared.[2]

Domestic sheep cannot survive for very long in the wild because of the weight of their hair. The long coarse hair protected their wild ancestors from a predator's bite reaching the skin and it kept them warm. The undercoat does not keep them warm, it weighs them down and it doesn't prevent bites from predators. Because humans have bred domestic sheep to harvest their wool, the sheep now depend on them for frequent shearing and constant protection.

Most shepherds move their sheep to the prime grazing areas at the best time of year. Untended, sheep are prone to eat all the food in an area and then will starve unless they find a new source. They need the shepherds to lead them to the best food and water supplies when they have exhausted the previous provisions. Shepherds also find shade for the sheep to rest in and provide oil to keep flies away.

When sheep are tired, they will lie down to rest anywhere. Without protection, they remain alert and nervous, which creates stress for the whole flock. Sheep that are stressed will often run from random noises, smells, or movement until they collapse from exhaustion. Since domestic sheep are valued for their wool, they have been bred to produce a coat so thick it weighs them down. The inability to stand up or run away quickly makes them easy prey for speedy predators. Dry, their wool can weigh several pounds, but if water soaks into it, they will struggle under the added weight. Moving water easily sweeps them off their feet and their coat will absorb so much water they can't stand up.

Wise, good shepherds will build dams to form pools with calm waters for the sheep to drink. This protects them from drowning as well as provides them with refreshment. They will find the best shelter from the weather and protect the sheep from predators. They will calm them and protect them while they rest. The sheep know and trust their shepherd. They will come to him when he enters their field.

When shearing or vaccination time arrives, many flocks come together, yet each sheep identifies their specific shepherd. The sheep don't go to just any shepherd,

---

[2] *www.sheep101.info/hair.html*, http://www.sheep101.info/hair.html.

only the one they have known, often from birth. They trust their shepherd to help them.

If a lamb, or sheep, repeatedly strays away from the shepherd, the shepherd may break one of its legs and carry it around until it is healed. This helps the lamb to bond to the shepherd and after it is healed the lamb will stay very close to the shepherd. (A broken leg causes the lamb to stay close to the shepherd…hmmm… Am I that lamb?) By carrying it around the shepherd can caress and love on the lamb. The lamb learns the gentle caresses of the shepherd. Along with caresses from the shepherd, sometimes comes discipline. The shepherd must discipline any sheep when it wanders off or heads in the wrong direction. He loves it and wants to protect it from harm.

Photo by joseph d'mello on Unsplash

Both caresses and discipline come from the shepherd using his tools: a rod and a staff. What are the differences between a rod and a staff? A rod is a part of a tree (possibly a root or thick branch) with a knob on one end. When shepherds are young they practice how to throw the rod. I truly think stick throwing is something every young child does, but for a future shepherd, this practice hones their skills. Shepherds throw the rod at any sheep heading the wrong way. The goal is to hit the sheep with the knob on the neck or head where there is less wool, so the sheep will turn around. This quick, sharp strike corrects the sheep and turns it back towards the shepherd. Shepherds use the rod as a reprimand or a form of discipline, but they caress and comfort with the staff.

* * *

Both caresses and discipline come from the shepherd using his tools: a rod and a staff.

* * *

The staff is a walking stick with a curve at the top. Shepherds use it to gently tap or caress the sheep as a sign of affection. The sheep learn to stay close enough for the staff to reach them. They are not fearful of the staff since it shows they are near the shepherd. The curved top can be used to help a sheep out of a hole by hooking around its body. Since it is used for positive taps and caresses, the sheep usually do not struggle when it is around its neck or body. Skilled shepherds use both tools to help their sheep.

I often say, "God hit me on the side of my head with a two-by-four." After studying the rod, I realize He hits me on the side of my head with His rod when I am too far from His path. He wants me to stay close to Him, so I can receive all that I need. He wants me to rest in His green pastures protected by Him. Now, this does not mean I always listen, but I am learning to listen and to remain where He wants me.

Jehovah-Raah, Our Shepherd, wants to protect me and bless me. He wants me to rest in green pastures. While storms rage around me, He wants me to sit with Him and relax. Our shepherd encourages us to rest, knowing He guides us. Jesus calls us sheep many times in the Gospels. He sends us like sheep into the world to share His gospel. In Matthew 10:16 Jesus says, "Behold, I send you out as sheep in the midst of wolves; so be shrewd as serpents and innocent as doves." Sheep need to be near their shepherd. Jehovah-Raah does not say we are going alone into the world, He will be with us. He is with us when we run into wolves or trials when we are tired, hungry, or having a great day. He wants us to stay near Him so He can protect us, and give us food, strength, and love.

* * *

Our Shepherd encourages us to rest, knowing He guides us.

* * *

He wants to anoint my head with oil and overflow my cup with blessings. Anointing is a representation of setting apart for the service of God. He wants to set me apart for His service. He wants to fill me to overflowing with His Spirit, with His plans, with His love, with His mission.

He anoints us to serve Him. He anoints our heads with oil. For shepherds, this is a common practice. They pour oil on the heads of the sheep to keep flies and gnats from getting in their eyes and noses and laying eggs. If the flies lay eggs, the sheep can get very sick and even go insane or die. Good shepherds anoint the sheep to help keep them healthy. Jehovah-Raah anoints our heads to keep us safe and to bless us.

He anoints my head with oil to keep away gnats that bother me. These gnats can be doubts, fears, insecurities, and worries. While writing this book, Satan kept planting doubts in my heart and mind. Am I worthy? Will anyone buy it? Am I sharing what God wants me to teach? The doubts, or gnats, of life, kept swarming. But Jehovah-Raah kept working and protecting me. Attacks came, but Jehovah-Raah was with me so I did not run away and hide, at least not every day. I learned that when I trust in Jehovah-Raah and remain close to Him, I stop doubting my abilities as a mom, teacher, wife, homemaker, writer, etc. I am still working on my biggest doubts.

One of the biggest is being an evangelist. In Matthew 10:16, Jesus says, "Behold, I am sending you out as sheep in the midst of wolves, so be wise as serpents and innocent as doves." As a Christian, Jehovah Raah gave me the Great Commission. He wants me to share the gospel with people around me. I am one of His sheep and I am to share His love with others. Yet the doubts about being hated, attacked and mocked come pouring in whenever I pause and consider sharing the gospel. When I talk to people my faith spills out, but when I stop to think about sharing my faith my doubts build up.

When I stop fearing for my kids, my husband, and my future, Jehovah-Raah anoints me with peace. He will do the same for you. Jehovah-Raah pours blessings over us and sweeps away the doubts, fears, and worries. His anointing cascades down from above like a river flowing over a waterfall, falling freely, completely covering all parts of us. His love washes away those pesky gnats, cleansing us from insecurities about our futures, our families, our callings, anything.

Back to Psalm 23. Verse 6 says, "Surely your goodness and love will follow me all the days of my life, and I will dwell in the house of the LORD forever." When I was little, I thought it meant I would never have problems once I accepted Christ as my Savior. What it actually means is that God's goodness and love will always be with me, but trials will come.

> *Count it all joy, my brothers, when you meet trials of various kinds, for you know that the testing of your faith produces steadfastness. And let steadfastness have its full effect, that you may be perfect and complete, lacking in nothing.* James 1:2-4

As I spend more time with my Shepherd, His love and goodness will wash over me. I will have hard times and trials but He will be with me. "He will not leave you nor forsake you." (Deuteronomy 31:6b) He will watch over us and protect us.

His love and goodness will never leave us; that is an eternal promise. Jehovah-Raah wants us to spend time near Him, to be set apart to serve Him, and to follow Him daily. Our faith in Jehovah-Raah can lead us into green pastures yet we may still traverse dangerous mountain passes along the way. Romans 5 tells us why Jehovah-Raah would lead us through those areas:

> *Therefore, since we have been justified by faith, we have peace with God through our Lord Jesus Christ. Through him we have also obtained access by faith into this grace in which we stand, and we rejoice in hope of the glory of God. Not only that, but we rejoice in our sufferings, knowing that suffering produces endurance; and endurance produces character; and character produces hope and hope does not put us to shame, because God's love has been poured into our hearts through the Holy Spirit who has been given to us.* Romans 5:1-5

Jehovah-Raah allows tribulations or trials so we can learn to persevere and grow. Our Shepherd wants us to grow closer to Him, more like Him. He sent us the Holy Spirit to teach us to grow. As sheep mature, they stay close to their shepherds, for protection, love, and blessings. We should desire to be close to our Shepherd. As Elohim, He created us to need a Shepherd, whose Name is Jehovah-Raah.

Jesus called us His sheep and even His lambs. Lambs are teachable and eager to learn. They will follow the leading of their mothers. They need to be taught to follow the shepherd and to trust him. Sheep are more stubborn and prone to go their own ways. Lambs will stay with their mothers and the herd. Trusting the shepherd is hard for young lambs. Young believers will follow the groups around them but it takes time for them to learn to follow Jehovah-Raah.

In today's world, people don't want to think of themselves as sheep. Many of us act like goats…butting heads with everything around us. Our society believes in "Just Do It". We are told all the time that we can do anything with our own strength. Many people believe no one should be trusted, yet Jesus calls us to trust Him. We need to trust our Jehovah-Raah. We don't need to "just do it" without Jesus. We need to do everything with Him. Trusting Jehovah-Raah can mean stepping out of your comfort zone to join a new group, or saying no to a job when you think you could possibly do it. When my daughter decided to do a semester abroad in Australia, I leaned on my Shepherd. His strength, peace, and comfort allowed me to sleep most nights.

Our Shepherd is a good shepherd. Another characteristic of a good shepherd is his desire to spend time with his sheep. Our Shepherd wants to spend time with us and desires us to spend time with Him in His Word. He will meet us whenever we turn to Him. Jehovah-Raah stays with His sheep no matter what, He won't leave His sheep. He promises this to Joshua and to all the believers who will come after him in Deuteronomy 31.

> *"Be strong and courageous. Do not fear or be in dread of them, for it is the LORD your God who goes with you. He will not leave you or forsake you."*
> *Then Moses summoned Joshua and said to him in the sight of all Israel, "Be strong and courageous, for you shall go with this people into the land that the LORD has sworn to their fathers to give them, and you shall put them in possession of it. It is the LORD who goes before you. He will be with you; he will not leave you or forsake you. Do not fear or be dismayed."*
> Deuteronomy 31:6-8

God is THE Good Shepherd, He will never leave you or forsake you. Good shepherds stand guard over their sheep at night. During these dark days, we need to remember that every trial comes through God, who limits how many we receive. Yet hard times are when God works in me and grows me. If I only faced trials I could handle, I would not depend on my Jehovah-Raah to help, strengthen, and guard me. When I am weak from handling hardships or trials, Jehovah-Raah leads me to green pastures with still waters to refresh and renew me.

Whenever we move, I know Jehovah-Raah will provide a perfect place for us with food, water, shelter, and security. I may not know what it looks like but I know He will provide. It may not be exactly what I want at the time but in the long run, it will turn out to be better than what I had wanted at the start. When we moved from Fort Jackson to Fort Sam Houston, I remember wondering how God would heal our family and especially my leg. He provided a house where I could heal physically as well as spiritually. I did not realize how exhausted I was from serving for years when we arrived in Texas. Jehovah Raah forced me to rest. Every physical therapy appointment I could make was in the middle of PWOC Bible study times. He replaced time with women with time with Him. He refreshed my soul and healed my leg.

Photo by mahyar motebassem on Unsplash

Good shepherds do not leave their flock without a guide or a protector. Jesus left us with a guide until He returns. He left us with the Counselor, The Holy Spirit. When I was young I went to a church that used the term Holy Ghost. For me the term Holy Ghost meant something scary, to be feared. Yes, we are to fear God but His Counselor is not scary. The Holy Spirit is our guide, our helper until Christ Jesus returns. He is part of the Trinity. He helps us by reminding us of scriptures and past lessons. He does not bring up past lessons for guilt reasons but to remind us of what we learned.

God does not want us to live with the guilt from our past sins. He wants to free us from our past sins and bring us forward. Living in the past because of guilt is not healthy. Jehovah-Raah wants us to learn and go forward living lives that bring Him honor and glory. Sheep do not live in guilt. I feel guilt and try to stay in that guilt but God wants us to learn from our mistakes and grow. We need to learn the lessons God wants to teach us and move forward.

Honestly, I am terrible at this. I have carried a huge load of guilt. As I grow in Christ I have been learning to leave guilt, hurts, pain, and anger at the foot of the Cross. I accepted Christ as my Savior in high school. While in college I wandered far from Him. I drank more alcohol than I should have, I did not go to church on a regular basis or have fellowship with other believers. When I was with my Christian friends during breaks I acted like everything was fine. In my heart, I knew I was far from God. But when my Good, Loving Shepherd carried me back into the fold, I lugged a load of guilt along with me. If I insist on wallowing in my guilt, carrying a load too heavy to bear, I'm not learning about His complete love and mercy. But as I spend more time with Jehovah-Raah, I am reminded that He has taken all those bad choices and died for them.

God loves us. No conditions. No requirements for perfection. God loves us. Just as a good shepherd loves his sheep whether they are listening or not, God loves us. He does not want us to live in guilt but learn from it and leave it with Him. He also does not want us to keep the hurt and anger of past wrongs and pains. He wants us to forgive others as He forgives us. He does not want us to keep living with the pain and anger. He desires forgiveness for ourselves and others. When we hold onto anger and pain we are not hurting the other person. We are hurting ourselves. Keeping bitterness, anger, and pain harms us and steals our peace. This leads to shame that can impede us from accomplishing the mission of sharing His love with others.

When we begin to cry out to God using the Name, Jehovah-Raah, we learn to trust him deeply. He will provide us with comfort, deep abiding rest, refreshment for our weary souls, and anoint us with peace and strength. He grants us forgiveness, teaches us through life's hard circumstances, and showers us with His blessings. Jehovah-Raah wants to give us rest and refreshment during our missions. He is our Good Shepherd, He never leaves us nor forsakes us, He guides us and provides for us. We must choose to follow Him like sheep follow their shepherds, to find rest and peace which is another Name we will discuss soon.

Prayer to Jehovah-Raah
Adapted from Psalm 23

Jehovah-Raah is my Shepherd,
I shall not want.
He makes me lie down in green pastures;
He leads me beside quiet waters.
He restores my soul;
He guides me in the paths of righteousness
For His name's sake.
Even though I walk through the valley of the shadow of death,
I fear no evil, for You are with me;
Your rod and Your staff, they comfort me.
You prepare a table before me in the presence of my enemies;
You have anointed my head with oil;
My cup overflows.
Surely goodness and mercy will follow me all the days of my life,
And I will dwell in the house of Jehovah-Raah forever.

Jehovah-Raah is my Shepherd and the Shepherd of my loved ones.
We shall not want.
You make us lie down in pleasant places.
You lead us through peaceful times.
You restore our souls;
You guide us in the paths the military sends us
For Your name's sake.
Even though my loved ones may walk in danger,
We will fear no evil for You are with us;
Your rod and staff give us comfort.
You prepare a table for us in the presence of enemies;
You have called us to be His.
Our table overflows with Your blessings.
Surely goodness and mercy will follow us all the days of our lives,
And we will dwell together in the house of Jehovah-Raah forever.

(Feel free to personalize this prayer with the names of those closest to you.)

Questions for Discussion
These questions can be used for personal study or group discussion.

"The LORD is my shepherd; I shall not want." **Psalm 23:1**

1. How are you like a sheep, ready to follow your Shepherd? A lamb, ready to explore but wanting the protection and provision of the Shepherd? A goat, not ready to follow the Shepherd but desiring to travel your own way?

2. When have you felt Jehovah-Raah's rod or experienced God's correction in your life?

3. When have you felt Jehovah-Raah's staff, or experienced His saving touch or gentle caress?

4. Have you ever felt like you were lying in green pastures? When life was wonderful, restful, peaceful? If so, describe it.

5. What gnats (enemies or distractions) are you fighting right now?

6. When has God carried you like a lamb?

7. List three ways you have seen God's goodness in your life.

8. What are your favorite verses on sheep or lambs? Think about David, Abraham…etc. I love John 10:11, it was one of the first verses I memorized. Choose one to personalize and write in the space below.

9. How will your increased understanding of God as Jehovah-Raah, empower your prayer life and equip you to carry out the mission God has assigned you? Write out a prayer to Jehovah-Raah claiming the promises and character of God indicated by this Name.

Notes:

5. JEHOVAH-SHALOM: THE LORD OUR PEACE

Photo by Nitish Meena on Unsplash

Then Gideon built an altar there to the LORD and called it, The LORD Is Peace. To this day it still stands at Ophrah, which belongs to the Abiezrites. **Judges 6:24**

Can you recall taking someone to the Emergency Room? When we were stationed at Fort Irwin, California, I had a frequent flier number for our local Emergency Room. It started 24 days after we arrived when my husband cut open his hand on Christmas Day and continued throughout our time there. My son sliced his head open twice–one wound needed glue, the other staples. The first time it happened he was pulling on a baton at AWANA. The other child let go suddenly and the baton flew back and sliced open his forehead. Blood everywhere, kids panicking, and in walks the Commander. Someone who is supposed to be calm, cool, and collected. Unfortunately, I was the commander of this AWANA program, so I fit none of those descriptions when I saw the pool of blood seeping from my son's head. The second time he was playing indoor soccer when he ran into the wall and his forehead found the only exposed bolt. Again, blood is everywhere, kids panicking, and up runs the coach. I bet you know who the coach was… yes, it was me. Again, I was not calm, cool, or collected.

Yet, each time I went to the ER, Jehovah-Shalom went with me. He gave me peace both times as I held my son to have his wound closed up. This Name means the Lord Our Peace. In the military community, we need to cling to this Name. As a mom of two girls and a boy, I need to cling to the Name.

> *"The Lord bless you and keep you; the Lord make his face to shine upon you and be gracious to you; the Lord lift up his countenance upon you and give you peace.* Numbers 6:24-26

How many times growing up did I hear these verses? At the start of every church service or something similar, I rarely cared. Lately, I have been seeing how this statement is a blessing from God.

Jehovah-Shalom means God of peace. We find this blessing in several places in the Old Testament. In the New Testament, Jesus quotes it in John 14:27: "Peace I leave with you; my peace I give to you. Not as the world gives do I give to you. Let not your hearts be troubled, neither let them be afraid."

We can also find Jehovah-Shalom in Leviticus 26:

> *You shall keep my Sabbaths and reverence my sanctuary: I am the Lord. If you walk in my statutes and observe my commandments and do them, then I will give you your rains in their season, and the land shall yield its increase, and the trees of the field shall yield their fruit. Your threshing shall last to the time of the grape harvest, and the grape harvest shall last to the time for sowing. And you shall eat your bread to the full and dwell in your land securely. I will give peace in the land, you shall lie down and none shall make you afraid. And I will remove harmful beasts from the land, and the sword shall not go through your land.* Leviticus 26:2-6

One of the common sacrifices from the system in Leviticus was the peace offering. It had to be an animal without blemish for a burnt offering. God and the person bringing the peace offering would then be in "peaceful satisfaction." Peace is shared between them through the sweet aroma of the offering. Although we no longer offer animal sacrifices, we can still enjoy the sweet aroma of the peace offering knowing Jesus' death on the cross gives us eternal peace with God.

Jehovah-Shalom also grants us peace when we keep His Sabbaths and reverence His sanctuary. Our weekly Sabbath allows us to turn to Jehovah Shalom to find peace. What does this look like? Keeping His Sabbath means entering into His presence. It looks different depending on the age of my kids but mainly it was time together to enjoy games, movies and usually food.

* * *
Our weekly Sabbath allows us to turn to Jehovah Shalom to find peace.
* * *

When we lived in Germany, I learned about Sabbath. German stores are closed on Sunday and they assume you will stay home or at least spend time with family. Restaurants are open but many Germans either stay home or spend hours at one restaurant enjoying the company of family or friends. As Americans we sit, we eat, and we leave, because we have things to do.

I learned to love Sunday afternoons. They were our Sabbaths after my husband preached or helped with the chapel service. Sundays, we spent time together as a family, not shopping or playing sports, just spending time together. My kids loved to play together, and they loved to spend time with us. The chapel family often sponsored potlucks after chapel to help us bond as a family of believers. Those potlucks brought families together and gave us time to talk with other believers.

In the past, many churches gave their ministers or pastors Monday off so that they could have a Sabbath. Now that technology has given people access to pastors 24 hours a day every day of the week, pastors are losing their Sabbaths. Many pastors who do not have a "Sabbath" burn out and leave the ministry.

By God's design, Sabbaths are days of rest. We are to spend time with God and rest. Some cultures do not even allow for cooking. God intended for families to rest together because when mothers and fathers demonstrate rest, kids also learn to rest. Often, pastors (and moms, especially me) believe the world will stop without us. We forget that Elohim created the universe and Jehovah does not change. He does not need us to run the world. The world will not stop without us, but we will come to a screeching halt without rest and peace. Jehovah-Shalom wants to give us rest through His peace. His peace is an internal and eternal rest. When we trust Him, He will give us rest.

When we returned from Germany, living in the Mojave Desert helped us slowly reintegrate into life in the US. Our kids were old enough to join traveling teams for sports, so Dave and I had to learn how to balance sports, chores, vacations, and work. We found ourselves busy every day of the week. We began losing our Sabbaths.

To combat losing our Sabbaths we began to purposely schedule time away. We limited the activities we signed our kids up for. Instead, we began taking trips with our kids. At first, I worried about them missing games or activities. Jehovah-Shalom reminded me to rest in Him and trust Him. Our kids wanted to join everything their friends were doing, but I could not be in three places at once. We allowed them to do one sport or activity plus AWANA. Those limits helped us carve out days when we had nothing scheduled. Those days helped us to recharge our batteries. Our Sabbath days were not Sundays when we had church, Dave preached, and the kids and I frequently pitched in with chapel duties. Often it was Friday evenings after school or Saturdays. We slowed down, laughed, joked, and enjoyed rest together.

Jesus and Jehovah-Shalom did not model non-stop work. Yet, for some reason, I think I have to keep moving and doing things all the time. Both Jesus and God took Sabbath rest. Jesus took time away to spend time with God. They, along with the Holy Spirit, spend quiet time together.

***

Jesus took time away to spend time with God.
***

Luke 5:16 says, "But Jesus Himself would *often* slip away to the wilderness and pray." Jesus knew the value of spending time alone with God. Often is the keyword. Jesus knew time with His Father was key to ministry. Time with God renews, strengthens, and sustains us.

Jehovah-Shalom wants us to rest and to give us peace. The more time we spend with Him the more peace and the deeper the rest He gives us.

> *Thus the heavens and the earth were finished and all the host of them. And on the seventh day God finished his work that he had done, and he rested on the seventh day from all his work that he had done. So God blessed the seventh day, and made it holy, because in it God rested from all his work that he had done in creation.*
> Genesis 2:1-3

Photo by Timothy Eberly on Unsplash

God rested after His work. He showed us by example to rest, to receive peace. When we follow the world's example, we find ourselves constantly busy with little or no peace. Look around at the world; conflict and strife abound. People spray other people with pepper spray for "deals" and attack one another over petty disagreements. When people do not take time to relax and find peace, they are more likely to be stressed and overreact. Following God's example of rest, equips us to bring peace to all that plagues the world today.

One of those plagues God brings to my mind when I read Leviticus 26:2 is technology. Even though today's technology didn't exist when Leviticus was written, Jehovah-Shalom had already made a provision for our protection from it. He wants us to have His peace and protection. God wants us to keep His Sabbath despite technology. Studies have shown kids who use technology every day are more likely to be stressed. Many studies show kids use technology to bully and harm others. When we choose to not obey God's command to rest on His Sabbath, we open ourselves up to more stress and less peace.

I try to unplug on Sundays. I still watch TV, but I try not to check Facebook or emails, which is so very hard to resist. I like to read and spend time with my family. While living in San Antonio, my husband and I would take Sunday night as our "date" night. We dropped our kids off at an AWANA program, then went out for coffee. We spent time together, reading books or talking. Many Sundays (or Sabbaths) we would talk and discuss things happening in our lives, catching up on dreams, desires, and hopes for ourselves and our children. Some Sabbaths we would just sit, read, and gain peace.

This "date" time was something my husband started. When we found the AWANA program, I assumed I would help out as I usually do. Instead, Dave asked me to say no to serving and spending time with him. It was wonderful, even though it may not have been what many people call a date. We didn't go to see a movie or eat dinner in a fancy restaurant. Instead, we sat together (quality time is Dave's love language). I learned to look forward to our time together. So much so that when we were asked if we would like to join a carpool and stay home some Sunday evenings, we turned it down. We knew we were not disciplined enough to avoid distractions at home that would keep us from actually spending time together. We chose to drive each week so we could have our date night.

Jehovah-Shalom blessed us both with peace. He wants us to be quiet and rest in Him. Times of peace do not have to be times of silence. As an introvert, I love time with Jehovah-Shalom. Dave is an extrovert, so being quiet is not his favorite activity. He finds peace by having praise music on.

***
Times of peace do not have to be times of silence.
***

A few years ago, my daughter Dena made a playlist for me that included the song, *Symphony* by Switch. The lyrics remind me that peace is possible despite the madness, the chaos, and the voices of darkness. I have had several opportunities to put this theory to the test as I have served in a variety of volunteer roles where I led women in ministry. Believe it or not, I have proven that it is possible to have peace when chaos swirls around me. Some people might find leading a group of women who love to chat chaotic, but it is peaceful to me because I know they are enjoying time together. Their joy is bigger than the chaos. God is bigger than any of the chaos we will ever face. Peace comes from having your heart right with Jehovah-Shalom. The more we obey God's command to deliberately practice rest, the easier it becomes to find His peace in times of chaos.

***
Peace comes from having your heart right with Jehovah-Shalom.
***

When we are distracted by technology, past hurts, or our To-Do Lists, our hearts are troubled. He wants to change us by giving us peace. By letting go of your past hurts, God can heal your heart and give you peace. He wants to do that, but we must let Him. When we cling to past hurts we don't allow Him to give us peace. Our stubbornness stops us from receiving peace from God. We must let God heal our hurts and change us.

> *Strive for peace with everyone, and for the holiness without which no one will see the Lord. See to it that no one fails to obtain the grace of God; that "no root of bitterness" springs up and causes trouble, and by it many become defiled; that no one is sexually immoral or unholy like Esau, who sold his birthright for a single meal.* Hebrews 12:14-16

We are to pursue peace with all men. If we have a problem with someone, we are to work it out, with the help of other believers if necessary.

Whenever we move, my heart defies the directions Paul gives us in Philippians 4.

> *Rejoice in the Lord always; again I say, rejoice. Let your reasonableness be known to everyone. The Lord is at hand; do not be anxious about anything, but in everything by prayer and supplication, with thanksgiving, let your requests be made known to God. And the peace of God, which surpasses all understanding, will guard your hearts and your minds in Christ Jesus.*
> Philippians 4:4-7

Jehovah-Shalom wants us to have peace, to not be anxious about anything, but when the Army gives Dave new orders, I usually start to worry. I become anxious about packing our belongings, choosing our new home, planning our travel, schools, and friends… You name it, I worry about it. After almost thirty years of moving with Dave, I have finally learned to take a day to fast. Fasting helps me to listen to Jehovah-Shalom. He wants me to remember that He has everything in His hands. He knows where we will live, how we will get there, who our neighbors and friends will be, and the assignments He has for us in that place. He knows all the important aspects of our move and wants me to rest in Him, to trust Him to provide all we need.

Through years of moving, my things have become less important. Being together as a family matters far more now than having our stuff. When we first joined the Army, I met a lady named Val, who had been in the Army for a while. She shared that they had just moved from Germany. Their household goods were put in crates and loaded on a ship to be brought back to the U.S. During the journey, the container carrying their crates washed overboard. They lost most of their belongings. For the insurance, they had to itemize everything. She did not know how many shirts, pants, and dresses she owned. As I watched her struggle, I learned things can be replaced. Even important sentimental items, like pictures and mementos, are just things. My people and knowing I will see them for eternity in heaven are truly the most important.

When we move, I have learned to lean heavily on Jehovah-Shalom. I want His peace to get me through my natural worries and my stresses. By having His peace, I can show people what the most important thing is, peace with God. But there are still times when I worry over small things, too. In John 14:1, Jesus says, "Let not your hearts be troubled. Believe in God; believe also in me." Jesus is telling this to the disciples at the Last Supper to prepare them for events to come.

When I ponder this Scripture, I realize I often allow the little things of the world to "trouble" my heart. Money, cleaning my house, my kids' schooling, extracurricular activities, or any number of circumstances I encounter on a daily basis cause me to worry about things I can't change. Instead, Jehovah-Shalom tells me to call on Him. When I take time to rest and fast, I find Jehovah-Shalom waiting to give me His Peace, which passes all understanding.

* * *

When I take time to rest and fast, I find Jehovah-Shalom waiting to give me His peace, which passes all understanding.

* * *

When my mother had open-heart surgery, I vividly remember what it felt like to rest in Jehovah-Shalom. Dave told me to spend as much time as I needed with her. Knowing he could handle things around the house and with our kids gave me peace. But Jehovah-Shalom really showed me His peace before, during, and after the surgery.

I flew from California to New York and joined my sisters who had traveled from Rochester and Toronto to be with our mother. My younger sister was very upset as the staff took my mother to the operating room. She is a very busy professor and having no control over a situation is very hard for her, so she cried and worried. I didn't have any more control over the situation than she did, but because I knew to cry out to God using his name, Jehovah-Shalom, I had peace. That peace helped to calm my sister down and gave us the chance to laugh a little and talk a lot despite our circumstances. When my mother came out of the surgery, I was able to stay six weeks to help her recover. Both of my sisters commented on how I did more than they had thought I could do. I truly believe Jehovah-Shalom gave me peace, strength, and a true servant heart to care for her beyond my natural abilities. My younger sister does not know the Lord. I believe my older sister knows the Lord, but she is not walking with Him now. Because of Jehovah-Shalom, I could become a servant so my actions might show Christ's love to my sisters, my mother, and all those I came into contact with during her care and recovery.

Just because I knew to call on Jehovah-Shalom for his peace in one situation, doesn't mean I always remember. I still struggle to enjoy His peace when concerns over my children's futures surface. I want to worry about things beyond my control and micromanage the details I think I can control. Jehovah-Shalom wants me to trust Him to guide my children. My children have to learn how to call on Jehovah-Shalom for themselves. He desires to give peace to everyone. Decisions about colleges, proms, careers, and relationships are all within His peace. I pray my children would learn to rest in His peace when they face decisions of any kind.

Jehovah-Shalom is the means of our peace and rest. In Judges 6, we see the story of Gideon. Gideon was a warrior from the tribe of Manasseh. His family was the lowest in the tribe and he was the youngest of the family, so every bad job no one else wanted fell on Gideon. But Gideon was smart and hard-working and one day God spoke to him while he was beating out wheat in the winepress in order to hide it from the Midianites. Gideon wisely wanted to be certain he was encountering an angel of the Lord so he tested the angel. When he found out the message was actually from the Lord he was distraught.

> *But the Lord said to him, "Peace be to you. Do not fear; you shall not die." Then Gideon built an altar there to the Lord and called it, "The Lord is Peace."* Judges 6:23-24

Gideon rested from his work and found peace in the Lord. But did Jehovah-Shalom stop there?

The rest of Gideon's story displays how he fluctuated between doubt and reliance on God in many ways. God told Gideon to attack the Midianites, but Gideon wasn't sure he had heard correctly and asked God for a sign. He placed a fleece out in the air and asked God to place dew on only the fleece if Gideon was to attack. The next night, just to make sure it wasn't a trick, Gideon asked God to make the fleece dry while covering everything else with dew. God did not get mad or frustrated. He understood Gideon's need for peace and assurance. And He understands our need for the same things, too.

God understood Gideon's need but He also wanted Gideon to learn to trust Him. When I am faced with a mission I did not see coming, I search for God's peace. When I was asked to serve on a local selection team for PWOC recently, I agreed. I felt at peace and spent time praying for ladies to step forward to lead our local group. The team met several times and we did not have any applications. Finally, we received one for the administrative coordinator and one for VP Spiritual Life. No one applied for President. The leader of the selection team asked me to pray about stepping down in order to apply to be President. I wrestled for two weeks trying to figure out what God wanted me to do. I did not have peace about applying, but the organization needed a President. I found my peace again when I stopped listening to the world and looked at the mission God had placed in front of me. After we interviewed the lady applying to become the administrative coordinator, the selection team all had peace that she should be president. Not me.

***

I found my peace again when I stopped listening to the world and looked at the mission God had placed in front of me.
***

When we were in San Antonio, Texas, God provided an opportunity for me to substitute at the local high school. I taught Chemistry and Physics for eleven years before I had children. After just a few days, I noticed the chemistry teacher was having problems, so I offered to help him. When he refused, Jehovah-Shalom did not give me peace about the situation, so I went to the principal. She said, "Since you think he needs help, why don't you substitute for his classes for six weeks?" I was shocked. *I knew this was NOT God's plan because I was teaching a morning Bible study and had kids who needed me. I asked God to have the Spiritual Life Vice-president say she needed me to teach the rest of the year (insert sarcastic tone here).* I was certain she would say she couldn't do without me, but God did not answer me the way I wanted. Instead, she said she would lead my Bible class for those weeks.

However, Jehovah-Shalom did give me total peace as I walked into the classroom. Several people, including my daughter Rachel, warned me that substituting for this chemistry teacher would not be easy. The teacher had lost control of all his classes, and his sixth period was the worst. Despite all the negativity surrounding this situation, Jehovah-Shalom did not allow me to worry. When I walked into the classroom, He gave me total peace and reminded me of everything I needed. I jumped right into teaching chemistry after 15 years. Sixth period, which was supposed to be the worst class, became a class where they loved to ask questions and learn. I expected to stress over having three kids and their activities and working full time. But Jehovah-Shalom gave me peace and rest, so it was not a burden. After the teacher returned, the principal asked me to substitute for him again at the end of the year for a week, and I jumped back in. Then, the school offered me the chemistry teacher job for the whole following year.

Without a prayer or a thought about God's plans, I signed my contract. Almost immediately, my peace vanished and I began to struggle in many areas. Our family fought and had many problems. Eventually, Dave and I remembered we should pray over our family and the situation. When we did, God gave us a very clear answer. He said, "Move." Less than a week later, we got a call to move to Fort Leavenworth, Kansas. We thought we were staying in Texas for Rachel's senior year, but God knew best. He said move and the Army moved us, which meant I had to resign from my teaching job. As soon as I did, my peace returned. I knew if I had taught the following year, I would not have been doing what God wanted. Jehovah-Shalom had a better plan for me.

Before I started my substituting job, I had applied for a fellowship to become an Accredited Financial Counselor. The fellowship was for military family members to learn how to help other military members with their finances. I applied in March and had to wait until June to hear if I was selected. I accepted the teaching job in early June and not long after got an email stating I was not selected for the fellowship. I was devastated. I knew God wanted me to apply for the program and I assumed I would get it because God wanted it. Had I bothered to pray before accepting the full-time teaching position, I might have noticed a lack of peace about that path, indicating it was not God's plan for the year ahead.

After we got orders to move and I resigned from the teaching position, Jehovah-Shalom gave me peace. Jehovah-Shalom had a better plan, I just had to wait for it. He also gave me the fellowship. I received a second email at the end of June offering me the fellowship. I was shocked but after Dave and I prayed over it (we would be moving right as I was to start the classes online), we both felt Jehovah-Shalom giving us peace.

* * *

**Jehovah-Shalom had a better plan,
I just had to wait for it.**

* * *

When we don't feel peace in an area of our lives, we need to call on Jehovah-Shalom to examine it and then follow His lead. We may think what we are doing is in God's will but sometimes we keep going straight on a path when God wants us to change course and do something else.

Before we went to Germany, I started an AWANA program at Fort Carson. I was the co-commander with my friend Susan. Working with her was fun and I loved this part of my week. At the end of the second year, I knew I was not to be the commander the following year. I assumed AWANA could not continue without me, truth be told I thought I was the only person who could lead it. Jehovah-Shalom does not want us to work with chaos in our spirits. Instead, God wanted my friend Susan to lead it. Jehovah-Shalom was taking me down a very different path and I had missed the turn. But lucky for me, God always brings me back on His path. He had chosen Susan to continue this program and moved me to Germany so I would not try to lead in her place.

***

Jehovah-Shalom does not want us to work with chaos in our spirits.

***

He wants us to trust Him, then He will give us peace and rest. He wants us to rely on Him and trust where He wants us to go. If we focus on the things of this world, we will not have peace. This world is changing and moving away from God in many ways. Focusing on the things of this world causes us to worry and lose our focus on God, but when we look for God and His peace, He gives us rest.

Martha in the New Testament is a perfect example. We meet her first in Luke 10. She is stressed over serving while her sister, Mary, rests and learns at the feet of Jesus. Jesus rebukes Martha for stressing instead of resting and learning. Later on, in John 12 we find Mary and Martha together again with Jesus. Most people pass right over verse two, but I am drawn to it. Here, the sisters host a dinner in Jesus' honor. Martha served, while Lazarus was among those reclining at the table with him. Do you see it, too? Martha went from stressing over serving to having peace from Jehovah-Shalom. She did not ask Jesus to make Mary help. She was at peace doing God's calling. She had taken Jesus' advice and sought Jehovah-Shalom. Martha is serving again yet this time she is resting while serving. She is not stressed. She has found her mission, her heart is at peace.

Like Martha, my mission is serving. Over the years, I've noticed my service is more effective when my heart is in the right place. While stationed at Fort Leavenworth, I was invited to dinner at the home of a dear friend. She was frazzled when I arrived. I instantly started to help. She needed someone to help with the last-minute details so she could focus on her guests. I just helped because God has equipped me for that work and I love my friend. She reminded me of that recently. She said that my "Martha-ing" helped her do better "Mary-ing." I allowed her to listen to God as she anointed the ladies gathered in her home. I got to rest and have peace while serving and still learn from her and God. She told me that by using my gifts I truly served her. I honestly do not remember doing anything much, but God used my small contribution to give her peace.

Jehovah-Shalom will give you peace when you are receptive. He calls people to do His mission here on Earth. When we call on God using His Name, Jehovah-Shalom, He gives us His peace. Peace not determined by our circumstances, our emotions, or any other factors. We can enjoy His peace on earth knowing God is with us. He has provided us with eternal peace through Jesus' sacrifice. We no longer need to serve to prove our place but we can rest from our mission by faith knowing Jesus secured our place in His Kingdom. Jehovah-Shalom gives us peace through the confidence that we are working within God's will on the mission He has for us. We can bring this same peace to all our relationships through reconciliation. Our relationship with El Elyon, The Lord Most High, needs to be where our focus lies.

Prayer to Jehovah-Shalom
Adapted from Psalm 4
To the Choirmaster. With stringed instruments. A Psalm of David

Answer me when I call, O God of my righteousness!
You have given me relief when I was in distress.
Be gracious to me and hear my prayer!

Jehovah-Shalom please give me peace. When I call out to you, stop my worrying and show me your great peace and strength.

O men, how long shall my honor be turned into shame?
How long will you love vain words and seek after lies? Selah
But know that the Lord has set apart the godly for himself;
the Lord hears when I call to him.

Jehovah-Shalom, protect me from lies and falsehoods. Show me the truth in all situations. Give me peace when liars attack. When I lie please show me how to make amends and heal relationships.

Be angry, and do not sin;
ponder in your own hearts on your beds, and be silent. Selah
Offer right sacrifices, and put your trust in the Lord.

Jehovah-Shalom, teach me to trust you. Lord, when I am angry, keep me from sinning. When I can't sleep please show me what I need to change and how to change my heart from anger to peace. Lord stop me from speaking in my anger.

There are many who say, "Who will show us some good?
Lift up the light of your face upon us, O Lord!"
You have put more joy in my heart
than they have when their grain and wine abound.

Jehovah-Shalom, give me peace and joy. Show me how to see joy in every situation. Guide me when I need to turn back to you. Show me your ways.

In peace I will both lie down and sleep;
for you alone, O Lord, make me dwell in safety.
Amen.

Questions for Discussion

These questions can be used for personal study or group discussion.

> *Then Gideon built an altar there to the* Lord *and called it, The* Lord *Is Peace. To this day it still stands at Ophrah, which belongs to the Abiezrites.* **Judges 6:24**

1. How do you see Jehovah-Shalom in the story of Abraham and Lot? (Gen. 13:5-18)

2. What does Psalm 29:11 say about peace?

3. Psalm 4:8 says we will lie down and sleep in His peace. What keeps you up at night? How can you release it to Jehovah-Shalom?

4. In Psalm 119:165, God talks about peace and His Law. What do you think of this verse?

5. Isaiah 9:6-7 is a prophecy about Jesus. How do you see Jesus fulfilling these verses?

6. Today there are lots of negative stories all around us. How does Jehovah-Shalom want you to respond? Name some practical things you can do.

7. Meditate on Numbers 6:24-26. Why do you think many churches use this greeting? Is there another verse you have used in greeting times in church?

8. How will your increased understanding of God as Jehovah-Shalom, empower your prayer life? Write out a prayer to Jehovah-Shalom claiming the promises and character of God indicated by this Name.

Notes:

6. Jehovah-Maginnenu: The Lord Our Defense, Our Shield

Photo by Risto Kokkonen on Unsplash

My shield is with God,
who saves the upright in heart.
Psalm 7:10

"Mom! Watch me! Watch me twirl! Miss Deb taught us another way to twirl in class! Mom!"

"That's beautiful, you twirled so many times! Can you show me again at home when Dena and Andrew are eating dinner?"

Her shoulders sank but she agreed. My shoulders sank as I realized I just destroyed a beautiful moment. Another parenting fail. Daddy would call tonight and she would brighten like the princess he told her she was. Daddy was gone again but this time was "only" 16 weeks away. Considering his six-month deployment the previous year, this "short" school was preparation for next year's deployment.

But 16 weeks of daddy gone is still 16 weeks of single parenting, which means doing everything for three kids ages six and under with no relatives living on the same side of the ocean. With my husband in South Carolina for school, I was left alone in a country where English was not the primary language. We had only been there for seven months when my husband received orders to return to the US for school. The Army does not think about families when they make decisions on schools. He left before our son turned one month old.

After a few more twirls and a deep bow acknowledging her fans, I started to load up the car with all the kids and their things. Rachel, my dancer, had to get in first since she sat in the third row being the oldest. Dena climbed in after her and got in her car seat "all by herself" which she would announce every single time. I placed Andrew's car seat in its rear-facing base. I passed out sippy cups and snacks after the girls buckled up in their car seats. As we left the dance studio, the bright sunshine and detailed rehashing of the class encouraged me. I finally felt my shoulders rise as the girls happily ate their snacks and Andrew cooed in his car seat.

Because ballet class was on post and we lived in a housing community "on the economy", our route home took us out a gate where a guard was stationed to watch us depart. The kids loved waving to the gate guards. Rachel played "who will wave at us" with Dena. The guards always looked bored and lonely. We never talked to them but my kids loved when they waved back. As I approached the gate, I was surprised when the guard stopped me. He tapped on my window and the girls were excited to see if they knew him. They shouted to ask him his name. Instead of engaging with very loud yet cute little girls, he looked me straight in the eye and said in the most serious tone I have ever heard: "Ma'am you need to go directly home! We are closing the base, NO ONE will be able to leave or enter."

One by one his words wrapped a tendril of worry tightly around my heart. I drove home wondering what his words meant. After unloading three kids, my purse, the dance bag, the diaper bag, and the weekly load of groceries, my arms were full, yet we were home. Home safe and sound.

Our usual after dance class ritual involved TV watching. But on base in Germany, TV consisted of three Armed Forces Network (AFN) stations, a few German stations, and two from England. I flipped on the TV for the girls and Andrew in a bouncy chair nearby where he could see me, the TV, and his sisters. Perfect! I could make dinner in peace.

"MOM!" bellowed Rachel, my still twirling six-year-old, "They aren't showing cartoons, they are crying on TV."

I came out to see the "TODAY" show replaying the collapse of a tower. Life came to a halt and the tendril of worry quickly started to twist and choke my heart and whipped me into a panic. I stumbled two steps from the kitchen to grab the back of a chair. The floor seemed to spin with every word the announcers spoke about the horrific scene unfolding on TV. I asked the girls to go play in their room while I figured out what had happened.

Slowly the anchor recounted the timeline of two planes hitting the towers in New York City. The station kept repeating the same video until the collapse of the first tower then both towers were lost to time in a huge cloud of dust and smoke consumed both towers. I drew a deep breath, expecting the dust to enter my lungs, instead, the tendril growing inside me split into multiple areas of worry and panic.

Then a third plane hit home, the heart of the military, where my father-in-law had served, a place people visited. I knew before I picked up the phone that a call to my husband would not go through. The noise announcing the lines were all busy was irritating and fed the vines sprouting in my heart.

I gathered myself by falling into a chair. I prayed and cried out silently to God. I hugged my son, who was babbling happily and called my girls. I started a VHS movie, calming the girls and myself, then I continued to make dinner. After I put the pot of water on to boil, I took time to pray. I thanked God for allowing me the time during dance class to get groceries even though carrying them from the car caused me to fuss and moan.

Soon my phone started ringing with local friends. We prayed. We cried. We tried to find out any information about what was happening in our adopted country. Servicemembers were not allowed to come home, they had to stay at their duty stations to prepare for the unknown. Attacking the heart of the military could certainly mean war.

I tried to call my family in the U.S. again. The noise announcing overwhelmed or down lines brought more panic into my heart. Defenseless, alone in a foreign country, and responsible for three young kids without any idea what would happen tomorrow.

What is happening? What does war mean? Who will help me? The thick vine of panic caused so many questions to race around in my head and my heart. How do I reach my husband? How do I find out what to do? When will I see my husband again? Why did this happen? Who is to blame? What will the future look like? The panic vines grew larger and stronger, full of doubts and chaos. They wrapped around my heart and made breathing hard.

I went to bed six hours after finding out about the attack. Worry and concern interrupted my sleep. I got up before dawn to turn on the news and learned about a fourth plane that went down in Pennsylvania. God sent me to my knees to thank Him for protecting our country from that plane, for the brave people on it who gave their lives for the actual target. I prayed for Him to help us, to protect us, to give me strength. I prayed for the vines of panic to be replaced with the roots of faith and peace. I cried out for God to provide me with strength. My prayers continued until dawn when the vines of panic began to wilt.

September 12, 2001 dawned absolutely beautiful, with clear skies and bright sunshine. I looked out my window to see God's answer to my prayers. We were surrounded by members of the U.S. Army, as we waited for the U.S. to wake up. Young Soldiers, seasoned NCO's, and officers guarded us, ready to do battle, wanting to avenge the deaths of the people in New York, Pennsylvania, and the Pentagon. They came, set up a wall, and stood watch as I slept and prayed.

God began to replace the vine of panic with the root of trust, peace, and strength. He reminded me of His protection, strength, and love. His shield surrounded my heart like the guards surrounded the buildings. Jehovah-Maginnenu, The Lord Our Defense, used the military to remind me of His never-ending protection.

Jehovah-Maginnenu means the Lord our Shield or the Lord Our Defense. Sometimes we know how He protects us, other times we may never know what He does to keep us safe. He works both in front of us like the airmen flying over the world ready to defend against another country's invasion. He also works behind the scenes like the Airmen translating communications from around the world. Either way He has protected, is still protecting, and will continue to protect His people. The Lord Our Defense defends us day and night.

Photo by Jason McCann on Unsplash

* * *

The Lord Our Defense defends us day and night.
* * *

God first revealed himself as Our Shield in Genesis 15. Abram has met Melchizedek, a priest of El Elyon and King of Salem, which means King of Peace. El Elyon is one of God's names meaning "The Lord Most High".

> *After these things the word of the LORD came to Abram in a vision: "Fear not, Abram, I am your shield; your reward shall be very great."*
> Genesis 15:1

God promised to protect Abram and bless him. This promise happened after Melchizedek blessed Abram. He announced His Name, Jehovah-Maginnenu, to show Abram other parts of His character–His strength, His protection, and His defense. God defends both individuals and groups of people. In Deuteronomy 33, Moses announced Jehovah-Maginnenu over a nation. He is the defender of the nation of Israel.

> *"Happy are you, O Israel! Who is like you,*
> *a people saved by the LORD, the shield of your help,*
> *and the sword of your triumph!*
> *Your enemies shall come fawning to you,*
> *and you shall tread upon their backs."*
> Deuteronomy 33:29

God is the shield around Israel; they are His chosen people. He protected them from Pharaoh's army and provided them with a shield as well as helpers they were not expecting.

As the Soldiers surrounded us in the days following 9/11, the vine of panic tried to regrow but Jehovah-Maginnenu used my kids and neighbors to stunt its growth. The kids and I spent many hours watching the Soldiers and praying for them. One of my neighbors grilled burgers and hotdogs. As we watched out our window a few days later, a group of Germans came up to the grill. We heard rumors that the Germans were marching to protest against America. The truth came out from this group who brought meat and sides to feed the Soldiers; the Germans were marching to SUPPORT America. They encouraged us to leave our homes without fear. As nations united to help America after the attack, our German neighbors united with us and encouraged us to return to life as usual.

King David, a warrior, and a former shepherd penned many Psalms about Jehovah-Maginnenu. The word "Maginnenu" means two different types of shields. One type is a large shield that can cover a man's body for protection. Roman soldiers carried this kind of shield and linked them together to make a strong defensive line. The other type is a small circular shield which can be used for both defense and offense. This type of shield reminds me of Captain America's shield in the comics and movies. Each one has a role in warfare.

> *But let all who take refuge in you rejoice;*

> *let them ever sing for joy,*
> *and spread your protection over them,*
> *that those who love your name may exult in you.*
> *For you bless the righteous, O LORD;*
> *you cover him with favor as with a shield.*
> Psalm 5:11-12

This Psalm reminds us Jehovah-Maginnenu is a strong shield who surrounds us. Just as the military surrounded our building after September 12, 2001, Jehovah-Maginnenu protects us with His shield. This shield is heavy and hard to move but offers the most protection. This one allows the people to rest behind the line, regain strength, or pause to regroup in the middle of a battle.

> *He will cover you with His pinions,*
> *And under His wings you may seek refuge;*
> *His faithfulness is a shield and bulwark.*
> Psalm 91:4

He protects us like a strong eagle protects her babies. This type of shield also reminds me of a mother bird. I remember watching the movie "Bambi" and seeing the mother bird put out her wings to protect her babies from the summer shower, as well as the mouse who needed shelter. Her wings shielded and protected her babies from the storm, allowing them to rest. The large shield can hold up other shields to protect from arrows above and swords or spears in front.

* * *

He protects us like a strong eagle protects her babies.

* * *

> *How lovely is your dwelling place, O LORD of hosts!*
> *My soul longs, yes, faints for the courts of the LORD;*
> *my heart and flesh sing for joy to the living God.*
> *Even the sparrow finds a home, and the swallow a nest for herself,*
> *where she may lay her young,*
> *at your altars, O LORD of hosts, my King and my God.*
> *Blessed are those who dwell in your house, ever singing your praise!*
> *Selah*
> Psalm 84:1-4

These verses remind us of other names, including Jehovah-Sabaoth, the Lord of Hosts. God protects and shields us and also commands His army to fight for us. Psalm 84 reminds us that Jehovah-Maginnenu shines bright as a sun, yet protects us from getting burned. He is holy and perfect, yet desires us to be with Him for eternity.

* * *

Jehovah-Maginnenu, our Defense, Our Shield protects us during every battle and skirmish.
* * *

Behold our shield, O God,
And look upon the face of Your anointed.
For a day in Your courts is better than a thousand outside.
I would rather stand at the threshold of the house of my God
Than dwell in the tents of wickedness.
For the LORD God is a sun and shield;
The LORD gives grace and glory;
No good thing does He withhold from those who walk uprightly.
O LORD of hosts,
How blessed is the man who trusts in You!
Psalm 84:9-12

King David reminds us God is our Shield and our Shepherd. Authors in the Old Testament knew the complexities of God's character. He is not one or the other, but all of His names all the time. Often, He shows several attributes simultaneously. Micah called God the Shepherd-King.

I will surely assemble all of you, O Jacob;
I will gather the remnant of Israel;
I will set them together like sheep in a fold,
like a flock in its pasture, a noisy multitude of men.
He who opens the breach goes up before them;
they break through and pass the gate, going out by it.
Their king passes on before them,
the LORD at their head.
Micah 2:12-13

Moses called Him, "The Lord Most High, the Almighty, the Lord, and God" in Psalm 91.

> *You who live in the shelter of The Lord Most High [El Elyon],*
> *who spend your nights in the shadow of the Almighty [Shaddai],*
> *who say to the Lord [Adonai], "My refuge! My fortress!*
> *My God [Elohim}, in whom I trust!"*
> Psalm 91:1-2

The prophet Isaiah called Jesus many names.

> *For a child is born to us,*
> *a son is given to us;*
> *dominion will rest on his shoulders,*
> *and he will be given the name Wonderful Counselor*
> *[Pele-Yo'etz], Mighty God [El Gibbor]*
> *Everlasting Father [Avi-'Ad], Prince of Peace [Sar-Shalom]*
> Isaiah 9:6

These verses remind me of Jehovah-Maginnenu and Jehovah-Raah, The Lord Our Shepherd. God often reveals different parts of His character in the Psalms. David reminds us that when our hearts trust God we receive His help. This help can come in the form of peace to rest during a trial or strength to fight in the battle around us. King David also reminds us in Psalm 28 to praise God. He reminds us God is with us in our battles but also with the nation of Israel. He again reminds us that God is our Shepherd who carries us.

> *The LORD is my strength and my shield;*
> *in him my heart trusts, and I am helped;*
> *my heart exults,*
> *and with my song I give thanks to him.*
>
> *The LORD is the strength of his people;*
> *he is the saving refuge of his anointed.*
> *Oh, save your people and bless your heritage!*
> *Be their shepherd and carry them forever.*
> Psalm 28:7-9

Before David became a king, he was a shepherd. He used slings to slay lions and giants. He fought with simple weapons yet God was with him and through God, David overcame great adversaries. He wrote many Psalms crying out to God to help him during fierce battles as well as when people verbally attacked him or lied about him. God strengthened him during battles and when he was emotionally and physically exhausted. God was his large, strong shield to rest behind. God is tender yet strong and mighty.

* * *
Jehovah-Maginnenu is tender yet strong and mighty.
* * *

The smaller shield is round and easy to use for both defense and offense. This shield can block arrows and swords but does not protect the whole body. It can be used to hit an opponent or break apart barriers in our way.

> *Blessed be the LORD, my rock,*
> *who trains my hands for war, and my fingers for battle;*
> *he is my steadfast love and my fortress,*
> *my stronghold and my deliverer,*
> *my shield and he in whom I take refuge,*
> *who subdues peoples under me.*
> Psalm 144:1-2

David reminds us of God's love. Jehovah-Maginnenu is our fortress, stronghold, and deliverer. He safeguards us and preserves us. How He does this may not be the way we want. When my daughter Dena went to college, we were hundreds of miles away from her and travel was a constant source of stress for us all.

My husband loves to make travel arrangements. He would book her flights not thinking about how short the layovers would be. I remember one winter break when God protected her mightily. She and her friend had to get from college to a nearby airport. A snowstorm delayed buses and canceled trains the morning they headed to the airport. They had to rely on taxis, and God sent many angels to help them. One was a taxi driver who would not leave the airport until he made sure their flights were still going. Their flights were the last ones that left that day. As she was traveling, I prayed for Jehovah-Maginnenu to protect them and shelter them from evil. He answered exceedingly. Both travelers made it home safe and sound, with a great story to tell.

Other Psalmists remind us to fear and trust Jehovah-Maginnenu.

> *O Israel, trust in the LORD!*
> *He is their help and their shield.*
> *O house of Aaron, trust in the LORD!*
> *He is their help and their shield.*
> *You who fear the LORD, trust in the LORD!*
> *He is their help and their shield.*
>
> *The LORD has remembered us; he will bless us;*
> *he will bless the house of Israel;*
> *he will bless the house of Aaron;*
> *he will bless those who fear the LORD,*
> *both the small and the great.*
> Psalm 115:9-13

God's shield can block arrows of the evil one. When we take refuge behind the shield, we find encouragement and strength for our weary souls. The flaming darts of the enemy come at us all day long. These can take the form of doubts and fears. *You can't move again, you won't find a job. No one will read your books so why write? You are failing your children. And letting your husband down You are a failure.* Satan uses these lies and more to distract us, paralyze us with fear, keep us from following God, and stop us from accomplishing His mission.

* * *

When we take refuge behind the shield,
we find encouragement and strength for our weary souls.

* * *

Finally, be strong in the Lord and in the strength of his might. Put on the whole armor of God, that you may be able to stand against the schemes of the devil. For we do not wrestle against flesh and blood, but against the rulers, against the authorities, against the cosmic powers over this present darkness, against the spiritual forces of evil in the heavenly places. Therefore take up the whole armor of God, that you may be able to withstand in the evil day, and having done all, to stand firm. Stand therefore, having fastened

> *on the belt of truth, and having put on the breastplate of righteousness, and, as shoes for your feet, having put on the readiness given by the gospel of peace. In all circumstances take up the shield of faith, with which you can extinguish all the flaming darts of the evil one; and take the helmet of salvation, and the sword of the Spirit, which is the word of God, praying at all times in the Spirit, with all prayer and supplication.* Ephesians 6:10-18

We are to "take up the shield of faith, with which you can extinguish all the flaming darts of the evil one." Our shield will stop the enemy's darts. Our faith in God will remind us how He sees us, and who we truly are. When we take refuge behind the shield, we find encouragement and strength for our weary souls. When God tells you to write what God has been teaching you, it does not matter how many books sell. When God gives you children, He does so because He knows you are the perfect mother for them. When the military cuts unexpected orders, God already knows the mission He has planned for you at your next assignment. And when He gives you a mission, He has already taken into account and overcome every way you might fail, all for His glory. Even when you feel surrounded by insults and injuries, He never lowers His shield of protection over you. His mission for my life may change from location to location and season to season. My mission will be different from yours and yours will look different from your neighbor down the street. But the end state of all our individual missions is to make God's glory known to all people.

* * *

When we take refuge behind the shield, we find encouragement and strength for our weary souls.
* * *

2 Kings 6:15-8 recounts the story of Elisha and his servant. They awake in the morning to find their city surrounded by Syrians. Elisha's servant is afraid, because the Syrian army appears stronger, with more men, chariots, and weapons. Elisha comforts him;

> *He said, "Do not be afraid, for those who are with us are more than those who are with them." Then Elisha prayed and said, "O LORD, please open his eyes that he may see." So the LORD opened the eyes of the young man, and he saw, and behold, the mountain was full of horses and chariots of fire all around Elisha.* 2 Kings 6:16-17

God provided a great host of heaven to protect Elisha and his servant. Just as He used the soldiers to surround my home after 9-11, He protected Elisha from the Syrians. Elisha asked for his servant to see how Jehovah-Maginnenu was protecting and defending them. Elisha prays for the Lord to strike the Syrians with blindness. He then leads the Syrians to Samaria in order to protect Israel. When their eyes were opened, Elisha had the Israelites provide bread and water, actually a "great feast" (2 King 6:23). The Syrian army returned to their homes. God used Elisha to bring peace and avoid a battle. God desires peace–peace in our hearts, our minds, and our spirits. This peace will flow out from Jehovah-Shalom to the people around us, our community, our nation, and eventually the world.

Just before Moses dies, he passes leadership to Joshua. Because he had disobeyed God, Moses was not allowed to enter The Promised Land. I have many regrets for my poor decisions, my short temper, and my strong will. I relate to Moses because he often was impulsive and his anger got the better of him many times. Yet at the end of his long life, he passes a blessing on to Joshua and the Israelites.

> *Be strong and courageous. Do not fear or be in dread of them, for it is the LORD your God who goes with you. He will not leave you or forsake you." Then Moses summoned Joshua and said to him in the sight of all Israel, "Be strong and courageous, for you shall go with this people into the land that the LORD has sworn to their fathers to give them, and you shall put them in possession of it. It is the LORD who goes before you. He will be with you; he will not leave you or forsake you. Do not fear or be dismayed."* Deuteronomy 31:6-8

In Joshua 2, Rahab the prostitute protects and shields two spies in Jericho. She has heard stories about God, and how He protected and provided for the Israelites. She hid the spies and then helped them escape. Because of her trust and fear of God, she risked her life and the lives of her family members.

> *And as soon as we heard it, our hearts melted, and there was no spirit left in any man because of you, for the LORD your God, he is God in the heavens above and on the earth beneath.* Joshua 2:11

Rahab did not know much about Jehovah-Maginnenu, yet she was willing to risk her life and her family to help the spies. Jehovah-Maginnenu delivered her out of

Jericho and her name is listed in the genealogy of Christ. She was a strong woman who desired to know more about God.

Just as Rahab risked her life and her family to help the spies, God calls us to let Him care for us and our families. Your children are from God, He holds them in His hand, rest and know you are NOT a failure. When my children were little it was easy to pray for God to lead them and care for them. Now they are adults, heading out into the big scary world alone to figure out life, I have been praying daily for them to know God. I talk openly with them about His different names and remind them of the stories of His faithfulness in each of their lives. I pray for Jehovah-Maginnenu to strengthen, protect, defend, and empower them to accomplish His mission. Rachel, my dancer on 9/11, is married to a man who has joined the Air Force. I don't know what their lives will look like but I do know Jehovah-Maginnenu will be with them, through trials and joy, through heartache and blessing. He will never leave them.

My new prayer for my kids, my adult children, is from Isaiah 41.

fear not, for I am with you;
be not dismayed, for I am your God;
I will strengthen you, I will help you,
I will uphold you with my righteous right hand.
Isaiah 41:10

Fear not Jennifer, for Jehovah-Maginnenu is with your children;
Do not be worried for Jehovah-Maginnenu is your God;
He will strengthen you and your children, He will help them and you,
He will uphold them in His righteous right hand.

When I start to worry, fret, and perseverate, over my kids, my future, my marriage, my *whatever*, I turn to God's names. They remind me of the Great Commission to share the Gospel as well as my mission to be a wife, a mother, a teacher, a trainer, and now an author. All throughout my life Jehovah, my Lord, has been with me. He never leaves me nor forsakes me. He is with me now, and will be with me in the future. His next mission for me involves more writing, teaching, and learning.

Prayer to Jehovah-Maginnenu

I give You thanks, O Jehovah-Maginnenu. In the world of social media, I sing Your praise; I announce Your love, wisdom, protection, and strength.

I bow down in prayer and worship You with my brothers and sisters in faith. Your steadfast love and faithfulness strengthen me. I lift up my voice to exalt You above all things, You are my shield, Jehovah-Maginnenu, I rest beneath Your wings. You are the One and Only True God.

Each day I call, You answer me; You increase my faith daily. Your shield protects me from enemy attacks. You draw me in to rest after battles and to rejuvenate me for the next skirmish. You pour into me; wisdom, strength, discernment, and compassion. You stretch out Your hand against the wrath of my enemies, and Your right hand delivers me.

Every day I call out to You to protect my children, near and far. Protect them, guide them, strengthen them, and lead them. Draw them close to You and increase their faith in You. Show them where to connect with other believers.

You are the Lord on High yet You see all Your children everywhere. Guide them and defend them, O Jehovah-Maginnenu. Guide Your teachers, leaders, and elders through their trials and the attacks that are sure to come.

Though my children walk in the midst of trouble, You spare their lives. The plan for their lives I give to You, draw them into fellowship with You. Bring them to salvation and develop their faith.

Jehovah-Maginnenu will fulfill His purpose for me; Your steadfast love, O Lord, endures forever. Do not forsake the work of Your hands, but knead, mold, and grow me into the person You want me to become. Knead, mold, and grow my children, grandchildren, and great-grandchildren to the seventh generation and beyond.

Thank You, Jehovah-Maginnenu, for never leaving me or my family.

Amen.

Questions for Discussion

These questions can be used for personal study or for group discussion.

My shield is with God,
who saves the upright in heart.
Psalm 7:10

1. Recount a story of God's protection over you.

2. What does Psalm 33:20-22 show you about Jehovah-Maginnenu?

3. Record how Psalm 18:1-3 describes God and what it means for you.

Description	Meaning for you
My strength	When I am too tired, He gives me the strength to get up in the morning.

4. When have you seen Jehovah-Maginnenu protect a family member? What happened?

5. In Proverbs 30:5, what do you learn about Jehovah-Maginnenu?

6. What story in the New Testament reminds you of God's protection or defense?

7. What situation are you currently facing where you need to rest and trust God?

8. How will your increased understanding of God as Jehovah-Maginnenu, empower your prayer life? Write out a prayer to Jehovah-Maginnenu claiming the promises and character of God indicated by this Name.

Notes:

CHARLIE MIKE: Continuing the Mission

"Who was it? I saw the rank...I know it was my husband. When will they come?" Every call started with these questions. A national news network showed the body of a Soldier from our unit, including unit patch and rank. Every spouse of those Soldiers called the commander's spouse nonstop. I answered because she was trying to get information from around the world. No one would release anything official, but every spouse held their breath while they waited. Once the family was notified, we could finally breathe again. I was able to keep my head and help because even though my spouse was of the rank, he does not wear his rank; he wears a cross.

As I drifted off to sleep after the notification was complete, I cried out to Jehovah. I know He controls everything and has a perfect plan, but I did not understand this particular scenario. How could this happen? All my questions and doubts drove me to pray for clarity and strength to survive this deployment, which had started barely a week before and would not end for fourteen more months.

God would not let me stop as I completed my first book on the names. He stirred the words for the *Call Signs* book when I broke my leg. That book is full of physical pain and spiritual growth. I was on a mission to learn more about Him. Through my physical and spiritual healing, I learned about so many of His names. Jehovah used this book to remind me of my mission–to share His faithfulness. Period. He is faithful, just, merciful, and entirely loving. He impressed my heart with more names and learning more about Him. He took me deep into the Old Testament and showed me wisdom from the New Testament.

This book is about the names God shared with me while writing my first book. Each one He brought up dealt with areas of my life I still needed Him to change. I needed to trust Him on good days, on bad days, and even on days when the bottom falls out of everything. To believe in His plan and know His timing is perfect.

After I finished the first book, I expected Him to stop showing me His names, but as my children are now all twenty-somethings, apparently, I need more help from Jehovah. He drew me into the desert to learn about Jehovah-Jireh, the Lord Our Provider. He reminded me of my time living in England and then took me to Jehovah-Raah, the Lord Our Shepherd. As I continued to learn about His name,

Jehovah, He planted a seed in my heart, which He tended. This seed grew into a mission.

That mission was a call to continue empowering women to call on the Lord according to the many facets of His character as revealed in His names, including Jehovah. Prayer is simply a means of communication with God. As believers, we have the privilege of calling on Him by name. There is a name that provides for every need, solves every problem, wins every battle, and comforts every pain. This realization inspired this book.

* * *

The more we know about God's facets, the more powerful and effective our prayers become.
* * *

My current mission is to write about the names of God, tell the people around me about His faithfulness, and share about His character and the facets of who He is. Jesus gave us the Great Commission in Matthew 28:16-20. He also gives each of us our own personal mission. Your mission will be different from mine and change over time. The more I learned about the facets of Jehovah, the more prepared I became for my mission. With the preparation also came attacks, setbacks, discouragement, and excitement. In every challenge I faced, God proved He was capable of meeting my every need.

In this study, we looked at Jehovah and then the facets of that name, such as Jehovah-Raah and Jehovah-Shalom. Each Name shows an attribute or facet, a part of the character of God. Even in today's uncertain times, with military deployments and civil unrest, Jehovah sees each of us and is with us. Jehovah-Jireh reminds us He is the Lord, Our Provider. Just as He loved and provided for the Israelites in Egypt and in the desert, He watches over us and loves us today. Many times, our circumstances make us feel alone—deployments, the heartache of miscarriage, loss of family members—but Jehovah-Maginnenu is waiting to defend us and protect us in every battle we face.

Learning about God's names is an ongoing mission for me. He gave me this mission over ten years ago, and I am still pursuing it. Along the way, He also gave me some short-term missions and a few longer missions. Every mission from God is part of His Great Commission.

> *"But you will receive power when the Holy Spirit has come upon you, and you will be my witnesses in Jerusalem and in all Judea and Samaria and to the end of the earth." And when he had said these things, as they were looking on, he was lifted up, and a cloud took him out of their sight.* Acts 1:8-9

Each mission in the military has many parts. Wherever there are "boots on the ground" there will be service members supporting them with fuel, food, intelligence, and vehicles. These missions rarely just use one branch of the service. Teams crossover to help each other. The Air Force can "Bring the Rain", the Navy can move massive amounts of weapons and people around the world. Just as a single military mission can take hundreds of people working together, Jehovah wants us to work together to share His love. His mission for you will be different from mine because you have different abilities, gifts, and desires. And He has assigned you precisely where He can use you.

As Jehovah, He gave me the mission of raising three kids to love and serve Him. There were days I did not think I would make it, but Jehovah-Raah saw my struggles and encouraged me. When I had nothing left to give, Jehovah-Shalom held me close and let me rest. This mission is not complete, it will continue until He calls me home.

To help me with my mission, God has taught me to fast and pray. Prayer is a daily need for all of us. In our prayers, we can ask Jehovah to reveal his plans and missions for the day and seek His guidance on how to partner with Him. Not all days will be easy and many times our circumstances will be beyond our ability to influence, but even in trials, our Jehovah is in control. Those trials pave the trails that can lead us closer to Jehovah-Shalom when we call on Him using His names when we trust we can rest under His wings and His protection.

Just as a good shepherd leads his sheep with love and dedication, Jehovah-Raah will be with us every day. He knows our missions and our heart's desires. Jehovah-Jireh will lovingly give us life-giving water through the Holy Spirit to renew our strength. Peace will come through Jehovah-Shalom as we walk with Him in the morning crispness or fall into bed exhausted from another day's battles.

Even though we are called to fear God, this idea is not popular, and many churches do not talk about it. People do not want to fear God. Popular culture encourages us not to fear anything. It is far more comfortable to only think of Him as Abba, Father. This view misses the bigger truth about God. He is above and beyond anything we can understand. His power and might are amazing. Because He is perfect, He cannot be with things that are not perfect. God wants us to learn *all* about Him and the totality of His character.

His names are characteristics, but He is so much more. He is the Alpha and Omega, the Beginning and the End. He wants us to learn more about Him, His attributes, and His whole Trinity. Focusing on just one part of God means we do not know much about Him. We need to continue to learn about Him to become more like Him. As this book draws to a close, I want you to know the names of God we studied together are not His only names. He is so much more. He has called me to continue to learn about other facets of His character. In the Old Testament, He is called Jehovah-Sabaoth, The Lord of Hosts, and Jehovah-Nissi, The Lord is Our Banner. The more I study, the more His Spirit reveals to me. This is a life-long process and our knowledge won't be complete until we meet Him face to face. But if we ask, He is faithful to provide us with a hunger to know Him more and make Him known in all the places He sends us and on all the missions He gives us.

As you read the Scriptures, watch for other names, write them down and learn about them. In the Appendix, you will find an example page to help you get started with your study of God's other names. As we look to God, He wants to show us more about His character and especially His love for us. Don't hesitate to follow Jehovah-Raah and rely on Jehovah-Sabaoth for strength. I am praying for you to find for your mission and to boldly seek God every single day. How is God calling you to make Him known today?

Jennifer

Sample Name of GOD Worksheet

So she called the name of the LORD *who spoke to her, "You are a God of seeing," for she said, "Truly here I have seen him who looks after me."* **Genesis 16:13**

1. Look up Hebrew, Greek, or Aramaic words translated to God using Strong's Concordance. Study the synonyms for the words you find there.

2. Who first used this name for God?

3. What were the circumstances surrounding this name?

4. Look up other Scriptures where the same words were used.

5. How are the people in those situations similar to or different from you? What did they need from God in their situation? How did He meet that need?

6. What might arise as you carry out the God-given mission that would make you call out to God using this particular name?

7. Who in your life needs to know the character of God as revealed by this name?

SMALL GROUP LEADER'S GUIDE

The following pages are designed to help small group leaders. This appendix includes what to do before your group meets the first time, a sample timeline for discussion, general information about the study format, and some warnings and helps.

What to Do Before Your First Meeting

1. Pray for Elohim to give you His wisdom and discernment as you lead women through the study.

2. Ask two or three people to pray for you during your time as a group leader.

3. Be sure you have good contact information for each of your participants.

4. Contact them before the first group meeting to see if they have any questions.

5. Dedicate a notebook to use as a prayer journal during your time together. Or you can use note cards which can be collected.

6. Either provide or suggest participants purchase a journal or notebook to record what El Elyon teaches them throughout the study. Plus, you can add other names as you find them.

General Information

Each meeting of this six-week includes a lesson to help participants focus on one Name of God at a time. Throughout the lesson, I have included some questions to process key concepts. Each week has a sample prayer and discussion homework. Keep in mind that you may not have time to cover them all. As you pray for your class and your lesson each week, highlight or mark the questions the Holy Spirit prompts you to be sure to discuss. Ask your participants if they had a question they particularly wanted to discuss or one they didn't understand.

As a small group leader, it isn't your job to know all the answers. It's El Shaddai's job. It is okay to say you don't know and then seek a study resource, chaplain, or pastor to help you learn the answer before the next meeting.

Consider some of the following for your first group meeting:

- Begin and end each class on time.
- Be sure to discuss the best way to communicate with each participant.
- Pass around a prayer journal or notecards at the beginning of class and ask ladies to write down their prayer requests or praises.
- Don't be afraid of silence. Give participants time to chime in before you tell them all the answers. Pay attention to who does most of the talking and invite those who are quieter to share their insights as well.

Sample Timeline
0900 – Open with prayer.

> Pass around the prayer journal or hand out the note cards.

0905 – Welcome the ladies to the Bible study.

> At the beginning of the first meeting, share 2-3 things you would like the ladies to know about yourself. Allow the ladies to share their name and one thing about themselves.

0915 – Give a brief summary of the week's lesson.

0920 – Share what impacted you most during the week's lesson. Hit the highlights that spoke to your heart.

0925 – Ask the ladies to share what impacted them.

0950 – Use questions to guide the discussion. Prioritize questions you'd like to cover as you work through each week's lesson. You know your group, so feel free to pick and choose the questions that would be most relevant.

1030 – Close your Bible study time in prayer.

APPENDIX A: *How to Read the Bible*

Studying the Bible for personal use is life changing! We are transformed by what we learn when we read God's word. We study the Bible to get answers, gain guidance, avoid wrong teaching, and to learn about Abba. Yet, our approach to the Bible matters:

- **Approach prayerfully.**
    Ask the Holy Spirit to use Elohim's Word to transform you.

- **Approach expectantly.**
    Expect to encounter El Qanna in His living word.

- **Approach carefully.**
    Read verses in context, asking who, what, when, and why.

- **Approach thoughtfully.**
    Record your thoughts and reflections.

When to Read the Bible
I like to read the Bible first thing in the morning to start my day, yet as a mom sometimes life starts earlier than I expect. You don't have to read the Bible just once a day. Anytime you have a few moments for reflection and meditation, the Bible is great inspiration—especially Psalms and Proverbs.

Study Aids
Many Bibles have comments and explanations. Read the Scripture first before turning to the notes. This method allows you to discern Adonai's Truth firsthand. A study Bible gives some background on each book and tells who wrote it, when and why. If you have questions or concerns, find a solid Bible teacher, pastor, or chaplain to help you. The Lord has gifted teachers who correctly understand and obey the truth. A good teacher helps us learn the right way to keep in step with Adonai.

Bottom Line
Approach the Bible prayerfully and humbly for a deeper understanding. Study verses in context and seek explanations from mature, seasoned Christians.

APPENDIX B: *How to Memorize Scripture*

Elohim's word is foundational to our spiritual maturity. Storing God's word in our heart means we have the truth whenever and wherever we need it. We do this by memorizing key and essential verses. Memorization allows Scripture to grow into our hearts.

Memorizing information, especially Holy Scripture, is essential. We must remember important information. A pilot can't always fly on autopilot, nor can a captain trust he knows where his ship is in the ocean. I understand it's not easy. Our memory muscles need development. But the more we use our memory muscle, the stronger it gets.

Tips for Memorizing Scripture:

- Find a quiet place, free from distractions.

- Read the verse(s) at least 3X: first for the eyes, second for the mind, third for the heart.

- Say the verse out loud—speak it with understanding.

- Write it down. Carry it with you and refer to it during down times (in line to check out, before a meeting starts, etc.).

- Read the passage at night before lights out. You will be surprised by what your mind does while you are sleeping!

Memorization can be a little frustrating at first. But the rewards are remarkable. Take your time. Memorizing helps us capture each word and remember it in the future. Being involved with the verse makes memorization easier. Other methods of memorization, such as using music, might help you. Repetition is important.

The goal is to let El Elyon's Word penetrate the recesses of your heart. Having a memorized verse spring up at just the right moment is encouraging and life-changing!

APPENDIX C: *How to Pray*

When we pray, we reach out to Abba. In the reaching, our attitude and spiritual awareness are changed. Abba is not a magician, it is not one of His names. Prayer is a relationship. Abba desires real and personal communication with us. He's more interested in what concerns us than how we pray. Prayer is personal.

In Matthew 6:9-13 Jesus taught his disciples to pray. Many people use this as a pattern for prayer, and others use it as a daily prayer.

> *Pray then like this: "****Our Father*** *in heaven, hallowed be your name. Your kingdom come, your will be done, on earth as it is in heaven. Give us this day our daily bread, and forgive us our debts, as we also have forgiven our debtors. And lead us not into temptation, but deliver us from evil.*
> Matthew 6:9-13

The book of Psalms is full of beautiful prayers. We can pray these back to Abba, or we can speak to Him and praise Him freely and personally. Though we can pray anywhere, Jesus often took extended periods of time and went to solitary places to pray. What should we pray about? Anything and everything! When you pray, remember this: Prayer is personal, it is talking to Abba!

> *Draw near to God and He will draw near to you.*
> James 4:8

- **Pray about everything.**
    There are no secrets with the all-knowing Adonai.
- **Pray with confidence.**
    El Qanna is not judging the delivery of your prayers!
- **Pray with thankfulness.**
    Gratitude is one of the ways El Elyon guards our hearts.

APPENDIX D: HOW TO BECOME a Christian

It means believing in the Lord Jesus for salvation. Believing Christ is God is an intellectual belief. Giving Adonai lordship of your life implies following His leadership—learning His ways and walking in them.

A Christian is a Christ-follower, a student, and a disciple. Being a Christian is much like being a service member because it requires faith, commitment, and trust. Being a Christian means surrendering to His leadership.

If the idea of being a Christian is new to you, consider the following truths:

> *'Jesus said to him, "I am the way, and the truth, and the life. No one comes to the Father except through me."' John 14:6*

> *'For God so loved the world, that he gave his only Son, that whoever believes in him should not perish but have eternal life.' John 3:16*

> *'For Christ also suffered once for sins, the righteous for the unrighteous, that he might bring us to God, being put to death in the flesh but made alive in the spirit.' 1 Peter 3:18*

> *'If we confess our sins, he is faithful and just to forgive us our sins and to cleanse us from all unrighteousness.' 1 John 1:9*

It simply takes a sincere prayer to be saved. You can use the following prayer.

> *Lord Jesus, I have sinned against you. I come to you today with an open and seeking heart asking you to forgive my sins. I believe You are the Son of God. You came to earth and chose to die on the cross for my sins, and then rose again so I could have eternal life. Beginning today, I give You my heart, my soul, my life to you. In the wonderful name of Jesus. Amen.*

If you prayed this prayer, please speak to your Bible study leader, a Christian friend, or pastor. They can help you continue to learn more and grow in your walk with God.

More Books by Jennifer Wake

Call Signs: How Knowing God's Character Empowers Women to Accomplish His Mission can be purchased at:

https://www.amazon.com/Call-Signs-Character-Empowers-Accomplish

Let's Connect

You can find me at https://www.jenniferwake.com

Facebook: https://www.facebook.com/mom23wakes

Instagram: https://www.instagram.com/mom23wakes/

Pinterest: https://www.pinterest.com/mom23wakes/

Twitter: https://twitter.com/mom23wakes

www.ingramcontent.com/pod-product-compliance
Lightning Source LLC
Chambersburg PA
CBHW082246090526
44585CB00021BA/2463